ORIENTAL
ART

India, Nepal and Tibet

for pleasure and investment

ORIENTAL
ART
India, Nepal and Tibet

for pleasure
and investment

By MICHAEL RIDLEY

ARCO PUBLISHING COMPANY, INC
New York

Published by
ARCO Publishing Company, Inc.
219 Park Avenue South,
New York, N.Y. 10003

Library of Congress
Catalog Card Number 79-123398
ISBN 0-668-02376-7

Printed in Great Britain

Contents

List of Colour plates

List of Black and White plates

Author's Note

There have been many books written on oriental art, both specialised and general. Most of these have stressed the historical aspect, paying little attention to the details of individual pieces and concentrating mainly on the great masterpieces and antiquities of the early schools.

Most collectors, however interested, will very rarely come across any of these pieces, simply because the majority are in museums, and should such objects come on to the open market they will cost a considerable amount, normally far more than the ordinary collector can afford to pay. Because of this, many connoisseurs and collectors have been frustrated by the lack of publications that tell them about objects that they personally have. Most books illustrate only the very best—masterpieces in their particular field. The same pieces seem to be illustrated in every book and the collector may find that he is unable to add to his knowledge about the objects he has in his collection.

I have deliberately written this book in a way which I hope will clarify many of the questions that collectors continually find themselves facing, and have tried to illustrate it, not with great masterpieces, but with objects that the ordinary collector will find that he can obtain, and may even, perhaps, have in his possession. I have, therefore, not included illustrations of major works. The collector, I am sure, will be able to find numerous books where they are illustrated. I have concentrated on the lesser antiquities and objects of the later periods. I have also included information which, to my knowledge, is not generally available to the collector.

I have tried to write this so that the information will be easily available and can be quickly compared with the photographs and line drawings.

The book is not intended as a great scholarly work. I am sure there are many others who can do this far better than I—but it is intended for the collector who simply wants to enlarge his knowledge of oriental art, and help him to understand better the objects that he may have in his possession, and also for the 'outsider' who may be interested but has yet to take the 'plunge'

INTRODUCTION AND MYTHOLOGY

A hundred years ago, in the days when vast collections were being made of art and antiquities from all over the world, this book would not have been written. Not because no-one knew about oriental art, especially of India, Nepal and Tibet, but because it has only recently become a recognised and respected art form.

As recent as 1910, in a paper to the Royal Society of Arts, Sir George Birdwood criticised a certain Javanese seated figure of the Buddha and compared it with 'a boiled suet pudding'!

Even those who had collections did not fully appreciate what they had in their care. An early statement in the official handbook of the Indian section of the Victoria and Albert Museum, London, stated quite bluntly: 'Sculpture and painting are unknown as fine arts in India'!

With this as a background it is quite a step forward for a book such as this to be published in a series aimed at the ordinary collector.

Collecting oriental art is now a serious and profitable pastime, one which the collector will find absorbing and financially rewarding. The subject is so vast and so deep that one is constantly adding to the store of knowledge.

This book makes no pretence. It is aimed simply at the collector who wants to *know*—a book in which the beginner will, I hope, find basic facts, enabling him not only to understand his collection better but also to add to it profitably.

Having said that oriental art did not officially exist 100 years ago, what, then, is it? What are its charms?

To some it may be a priceless gilt-bronze figure of the Buddha, seated in the splendour of a display case in a museum. To others it may be just another piece of 'junk', the 'wog gear' of some back-street dealer. It can be everything, or nothing—but it is just that much more if one knows something about it, especially the many stories connected with the gods and goddesses that are so frequently represented.

The three gods of the Hindu trinity, Brahma, Vishnu and

Siva, were among the most popular of subjects depicted in Indian art. Brahma is the Creator of the Universe, Vishnu, the Preserver, and Siva, the Destroyer. Although they are meant to be one being, the worship of them grew into various cults, which attempted to establish the supremacy of one or another. Cults grew up, dedicated to the worship of Vishnu, and others to the worship of Siva. The incarnations and manifestations of both also attracted sub-sects, all of which produced and dedicated temples, images and sculptures to the worship of the deity.

Brahma is represented with four heads. Originally he was said to have had five, but one was cut off by Siva—a story obviously favoured by the devotees of Siva. In pictures he is coloured red. His vahana or mount, is the goose. The Vedas are said to have originated from one of his heads. Brahma is also known as Prajapati—Lord of Creatures. His consort is Sarasvati, who is thought of as the patroness of music and poetry.

Vishnu is often represented sleeping on the coils of the serpent Shesha. His wife sits at his feet and the stem of a lotus grows from his navel, with Brahma sitting in the blossom. He has four arms and hands, in which he holds his attributes: the conch shell, the wheel, the mace and the lotus. His vahana, or mount, is Garuda. His colour is black. Another common form of the god, often shown in bronzes, depicts him standing upright, holding his four symbols.

There are a thousand names for Vishnu. They are usually strung together in verse, and muttered by devotees as a litany, which gives absolution from sin, and other benefits.

The power of Vaishnavas (devotees of Vishnu) was very great. There is a story in the Vishnu Purana, which tells of Yama, the God of Death, saying to one of his deputies that he was lord of all men, except the Vaishnavas—in a way pointing to spiritual liberation by the worship of Vishnu.

Vishnu can be worshipped as a single deity or jointly with his consort, Lakshmi, or as in one of his incarnations.

Lakshmi is the Goddess of Wealth. When Vishnu assumed incarnations, Lakshmi accompanied him. As Sita, she accompanied Vishnu as Ramachandra, and as Rukmini, she accompanied him as Krishna.

The cult of Vishnu is very complex. There are ten incarnations, or avatars, of Vishnu, each of which has its own devotees. It is interesting to note that the Buddha is honoured by the Hindus as a major incarnation of the god.

Vishnu, as Preserver of the Universe, had to leave his celestial world to be re-born, in order to destroy evil and preserve righteousness. On these occasions he manifested himself in different incarnations. These avatars, or incarnations, are numerous but there are ten important ones. They are: Matsya, or fish; Kurma, or tortoise; Varaha, or boar; Narasimha, or man-lion; Vamana, or dwarf; Parasurama, or militant Brahmin; Ramachandra; Krishna; Buddha; and Kalki.

Krishna's brother, Balarama, is also mentioned in the Puranas as an avatar of Vishnu.

The incarnations, Matsya, Kurma, Varaha, Narasimha and Vamana are said to have taken place on other worlds; Parasurama, Ramachandra, Krishna and Buddha, on this world; and Kalki is the future form that Vishnu will take at the end of the world.

Krishna was, perhaps, one of the most popular of the avatars. Vishnu assumed the form of Krishna in order to kill the demon, Kansa, who was born of the union between a demon and the beautiful wife of Ugrasena, king of Muthara. Kansa was so evil that the earth itself revolted, and in the form of a cow, petitioned the gods to help. The gods took her to Brahma, who took her to Siva, who, in his turn, took her to Vishnu, who promised to save the earth and destroy Kansa. Krishna is probably best known for his exploits with the gopis or milkmaids.

There are some weird and wonderful stories told about Siva, most of them having some bearing upon his many iconographic representations. He is one of the oldest of the gods and was probably an adaptation of a pre-Aryan deity. There are seals found in the Indus Valley, that have representations on them, which some scholars believe to be an early pictorial form of Siva.

Siva's appearance is unusual. He is represented as an ascetic, with matted hair, and with a third eye on his forehead. His hair is tied with the coil of a snake, which spreads its hood over his head. He wears another snake around his neck, with a third one which serves as the sacred thread.

When painted or in coloured images, he is shown white but with a black neck. The story of the black neck is rather interesting. The tale goes that a serpent, which Siva was using to churn the milk ocean, vomited poison, which Siva drank, to prevent it from contaminating the celestial nectar. Parvati, Siva's wife, on seeing this, choked him, causing the poison to get stuck in his

Colour Plate
1. A very large solid bronze Dipa–Lakshmi figure. South India. 18th century. Ht. 95 cm.

16

1. Bronze image of Vishnu, sleeping on the coils of the serpent Shesha, the stem of a lotus grows from his navel, with Brahma sitting in the blossom. South India. 18th–19th century. Ht. 7 cm.

2. Bronze icon of Garuda. Deccan. 18th–19th century. Ht. 8 cm.

Colour Plate
2. Jungli folk Bronze figure of a god riding a peacock. Probably Subrahmanya. 19th century. Ht. 20 cm.

3. Bronze image of Lakshmi–Narasimha. Vishnu in his lion avatar with his consort Lakshmi. His legs are in the Yogasana and supported by the yogapatta. Deccan. 19th century. Ht. 11 cm.

throat, turning his neck black.

In his war-like form Siva holds a trident. A popular image shows him as Nataraja, Lord of the Dance, which symbolises the constant motion of the universe. Siva dances in joy and in sorrow. As Nataraja he dances on the dead body of the enemy

4. Bronze figures of Radha and Krishna as Venugopala. Eastern India. 18th century. Ht. 18 cm.

5. Bronze figure of Siva Pasapata-murti, four-armed with Pasa, Trisula, and Yapala. Bihar. 18th century. Ht. 14 cm.

6. Bronze Siva Lingam with naga canopy. 18th–19th century. Ht. 8 cm.

of the gods—a symbolic dance of the triumph of good over evil.

Like Vishnu, Siva, too, has a thousand names, one of the most popular of which is Mahadeva—Great God.

A widely worshipped form of Siva is the lingam, the phallic symbol.

Saivas distinguish themselves by a caste mark of three horizontal lines on the forehead. The lower castes of devotees, the fakirs, and so on, practise self-torture, some of them literally walking themselves to death, symbolising the belief in perpetual motion.

Sati, Siva's consort, committed suicide by throwing herself into the fire in order to vindicate her husband's honour in an argument with her father. Siva was so infuriated and overcome with grief that in a fit of madness he began to dance and dance, until he had danced around the world seven times, carrying with him Sati's body. Vishnu, afraid of what Siva's dance might lead to, dismembered Sati into fifty pieces, which fell on different parts of the earth. Sati was later re-born as Uma, daughter of the Himalayas, otherwise known as Parvati. Siva and Parvati are often depicted together, sometimes with Parvati sitting on Siva's knee.

Durga is supposed to be the horrific aspect of Parvati, although she can be said to be the energy of Siva, redirected. The Puranas relate that Durga was born from 'the radiant flames that issued from the mouths of Brahma, Vishnu and Siva, as well as from the mouths of other principal deities'. Her aim was to kill Mahisha, the buffalo demon. As Durga she is shown with ten arms, in which she holds the emblems of the power of the gods. She is said to have received the name of Durga from having killed a demon of that name.

Iconographically, Durga is depicted as a woman with gentle expression and with ten arms, each of which holds a weapon. One foot rests on the body of Mahisha and the other on her vahana, the lion, which is shown mauling Mahisha's body.

Parvati, in her terrific aspect, is shown as Kali, the black goddess, who is said to have destroyed time itself. At one period it was customary to hold human sacrifices to her. In the Kalika Purana, Siva tells his sons that a human sacrifice will please Devi for a thousand years, and a sacrifice of three men, for a hundred thousand years. Iconographically she is represented as half-naked, wearing a garland of skulls, her tongue hanging out of her mouth, which is dripping with blood.

Because the gods feared the union of Siva and Parvati they asked him not to have children. Without Parvati's knowledge, Siva consented, but when Parvati found out she was so enraged that she cursed the wives of the other gods to remain barren like herself. So, in Indian mythology, none of the goddesses could bear children. The sons and daughters of the gods, therefore, are mind children or produced in some celestial way.

There are many stories that tell of the 'birth' of Ganesha. One says that Parvati formed him from the oil and ointments from the bath, together with her body impurities, and used him to guard her bath. Siva, not knowing of this, tried to enter the bathing chamber but could not force his way past Ganesha. In the fight that broke out, Siva cut off Ganesha's head. When Parvati found out what had happened she was overcome with grief, and in order to conciliate her, Siva ordered to be brought to him the head of the first living being that was found. It so happened that this was an elephant. Hence, Ganesha has an elephant's head.

There is another story which says that Parvati so wanted a son that Vishnu himself took on the form of a child and became her son. When all the gods came to congratulate Parvati and to look at her child she noticed that one, Sani, refused to look upon him, saying that he was cursed and that if he looked upon the child it would die. Thinking that her son was immune, she bade him look at him, with the result that Ganesha's head was severed from its body. This time it was Vishnu who set out on his mount, Garuda, to find another head for the child, in order to console her, and again, the head he found was an elephant's.

Ganesha is a very popular god in India and is even represented iconographically in Tibet and Nepal. He is sometimes shown riding on his vahana, a rat.

Other gods of the Hindu Pantheon include Kartikeya, God of War, and Indra, who, in Vedic times, was an extremely important deity and was thought of as God of Rain and Lightning. Later in the Puranas he is given a place subordinate to members of the Trinity and their consorts and sons. His weapon is the vajra, the thunderbolt.

Agni, the God of Fire, was, in Vedic times, second in importance to Indra, but in the Puranas is given a subordinate position. He is also sometimes associated with Surya, the Sun.

Another Vedic god was Varuna, whose vahana was the monster fish, Makara.

The God of Death was Yama, whose position in the Hindu Pantheon was similar to that of Pluto in Greek mythology.

Kubera was the God of Wealth.

There are, of course, in addition to the gods and goddesses previously described, numerous gandharvas, apsaras, demigods and rishis, including Hanuman, the monkey god, who was born of an apsara, but was transformed into a monkey by a

7. Bronze figure of Ganesha. Deccan. 19th century. Ht. 17 cm.

curse.

It will be obvious from the above that the Hindu religion is very complicated but extremely interesting, and it is well worth the effort to understand the background of the various iconographic representations, as it adds greatly to the enjoyment derived from collecting oriental art.

Buddhism was born early on in the development of Indian culture and itself has many legends, both of the life of Gautama, the Buddha, and the Jatakas, his previous lives. These provide a great deal of the inspiration of early Buddhist art. The early Buddhist doctrine was known as the Hinayana, the Small Vehicle. This orthodox sect was based on doctrine, rather than the worship of the Buddha.

Mahayana Buddhism, the Great Vehicle, was a later development and incorporated the worship of the Buddhas and Bodhisattvas. The Bodhisattva was worshipped as one who could intercede on behalf of a devotee. In order to do this, he had to sacrifice Nirvana, or the attainment of Buddha-hood.

A later form of Buddhism, formed in the 6th century A.D., was based on the Tantras, treatise on the worship of the Sakti and the Attainment of Perfection or the eight Siddhis. The Sakti is the energy of the god, usually expressed as female. It was this form of Buddhism that was imported into Tibet and formed the basis of Lamaism. There was also a form of Tantric Hinduism.

The third important religious force, Jainism, was founded by Vardhamana or Mahavira, a historical figure, the second son of Siddhartha, a chieftain of the Republic of Vaisali in Bihar. He was thought to be born in the year 599 B.C., though a rival sect believed he was born sixty years earlier. He decreed that the Jain community should be divided into four: monks and nuns, laymen and laywomen. He also decreed that one should not take life, and therefore banned the eating of meat and the use of animal products. The Jains do not believe in God but in gods and demons. The greatest beings are Tirthankaras, or liberated souls, who have once been world teachers. There are twenty-four Tirthankaras, the twenty-fourth being Mahavira.

Mohammedanism is, of course, a foreign religion to India but one which has played a vital role in Indian art.

It will be seen from the foregoing that religion in oriental art is a major factor, and, with some notable exceptions, art for art's sake does not occur in the Orient but is a necessary instrument and by-product of religion, in much the same way as the major works of art of the medieval period in the West were directly due to religious stimuli.

The massive sub-continent of India and, additionally, the

geographical areas of Tibet and South-East Asia, together house four main religions: Hinduism, Jainism, Buddhism and Mohammedanism. However, within these religions there are many sects, and each of these sects at different periods, and at different places, had a major influence on the artistic development of regions. In order to appreciate oriental art it is essential to understand the basic stimuli on the arts and therefore it is necessary to consider the mythology and religious texts which directly affect the production of sculpture, stone and bronze, paintings, architecture and associated works of art.

The fundamentals which, together, form the complex religion of Hinduism, come from many different spheres. Firstly, there are the basic tribal agricultural deities, which were worshipped long before the formalisation of the Vedic religion, but which have since taken on formal Vedic names. The Vedic religion, itself, is the result of an early influx of the Aryan invaders into India after the fall of the great cities of the Indus Valley. As an Indo-European religion, there are many aspects which are identical to other religions of the Indo-European family. However, in India, as in many other countries, environment has played its part in forming something which is typically Indian, but which, nevertheless, during later periods, was exported by missionaries to such places as Indo-China, Java, etc. The influence of Buddhism, too, was very great, and is found in India, Nepal, Tibet, South-East Asia, China and Japan.

Art, therefore, is the servant of religion. In India it was the major stimulus responsible for the erection of great temples; works of sculpture, which decorated the exterior of these buildings and which formed an integral part of the architecture; and images in metal, which were worshipped in temples, carried in religious ceremonies and kept in homes in personal shrines. The creation of beauty, in fact, was a form of worship.

Painting, too, was inspired by religion in early times, and even in later days it formed a major impetus in the production of miniature paintings of the Hindu schools.

The force of religion as a stimulus to art can, perhaps be best seen in Tibet, where the whole society revolves around religious and philosophical ideas.

In a land as large as India, although the religious stimuli may be the same in various parts of the sub-continent, the expression of the ideas will differ regionally, due to another important factor: environment. Environment, in fact, plays a major role in the over-all appearance of art styles throughout the sub-continent. It is possible to see foreign influences upon Indian art, but they are very quickly assimilated and 'Indianised'. Foreign ideas, therefore, can easily be expressed in typical indigenous ways. The artists and craftsmen in India, Nepal and Tibet were traditionalists and extremely conservative. Their craft had usually been passed down over generations and conformed to strict canons, which dictated the form of practically everything. It is obvious, then, that with a background such as this, the stylistic development over the centuries was slow and deliberate. It remained, in fact, typically Indian or Tibetan, as the case might be, with an over-all 'national appearance'.

INDIAN BRONZE SCULPTURE

In India, according to tradition, an artist was not considered accomplished until he could draw, paint and work with equal dexterity in eight different materials—stone, terracotta, wood, stucco, metal, ivory, sugar, and an unknown substance called Yantra. This made him extremely versatile, the tradition being evident even in the most decadent art.

Probably the greatest achievement of the Indian artist was his ability to produce figures of his gods in bronze, often creating the most fantastic of shapes in a realistic and life-like way and at the same time adhering to a rigid code which laid down his every move.

The Indian bronze is, in fact, a misnomer, for the figures are rarely made from bronze but from brass or copper, 'bronze', however, being the collective name for the figures as a whole. It is often very difficult to distinguish what the metal of a particular figure is.

Metal was used for casting statuettes in India from prehistory—the earliest known figure being a small bronze statuette of a dancing girl found in the Indus city of Mohenjo daro—now in Pakistan. The method the craftsman used to produce this figure is the same as was used later during the Medieval period and which is still used to this day: the cire perdue or lost wax method.

Indeed, as one studies Indian art one is constantly struck by the conservatism of the people. Nothing is changed—new ideas are assimilated, but the old ones are not discarded; they exist and blend with the new. This often brings violent contradictions but somehow the two manage to survive happily side by side.

It is possible today to see terracotta figures made by village craftsmen who have never left their villages or seen any of the wondrous works of art uncovered from the great buried cities of the past, and yet these figures will often be similar to those which have been made centuries ago. This illustrates the acute conservatism of the Indian artist, where a particular skill may have been handed down from father to son over many hundreds of years.

In ancient India metal was used in many forms—both pure metals and alloys being used. In one of the ancient Vedic Hymns, the Yagar Veda, it is mentioned that gold, silver, lead, tin and iron were used.

The most common form of Indian bronze consisted of an alloy of copper and tin in the ratio ten to one, although the use of pure copper for the production of religious figures was very common from the earliest times.

Apart from the little bronze figure of the dancing girl from Mohenjo-daro, no other bronze figure of merit has been found which dates before the Christian era.

Later, during the Gupta period, many large and grand figures were made, often in gold and silver and inlaid with precious stones. None of these have been found but several of the larger bronze figures are known.

To understand fully the various stylistic changes that occur in Indian sculpture, both bronze and stone, it is necessary to appreciate the importance of geography.

As a geographical entity, India is gigantic; not only a country but almost a continent. It embraces many races of people and many extremes of climate, which contribute in their way to the over-all 'image' of Indian art. When the historical element is introduced on to the geographical background it weaves a most complex web, which principally affects the development of Indian bronze art.

In the North, practically no significant examples of bronze statuary are found which date before the great Gupta dynasty (4th to 6th century A.D.). The Gupta period produced magnificent bronze figures, mostly of large size (at least, most of the surviving examples are large). Most of these were in the traditional styles of the artistic centres of that time—Sarnath or Mathura. There is a very fine standing figure of the Buddha, which dates to this period, found at Sultangunj, which is now in the Birmingham Museum.

The metal sculpture of the Gupta period was the result of changes in the style of the earlier Gandhara phase and the classical traditions, thus forming a standard which widely

27

influenced later artists. This can be seen in a comparison of the stone sculpture from Gandhara, Mathura and Sarnath. The long curls of the Buddha's hair have become symbolic tight snailshell curls. The drapery has lost its Mediterranean classical realism and becomes mere suggestion and, above all, the features have lost their foreign influence and become pure Indian. Gupta sculpture was made to harmonise with the architecture of the time, decorative patterns merging with the intricate lines of the buildings.

After the decline of the Gupta empire, there followed a period of internal strife, and chaos reigned, until in A.D. 606 a king named Harsha gained control. He was a Buddhist and gave every encouragement to the proliferation of Buddhist art. Unfortunately, practically no sculpture survives which can be attributed to the forty-one years of Harsha's reign. He continued the practice of enriching temples with treasures and works of art, a tradition which both Buddhist and Hindu priests encouraged. Countless works of art were given to the temples, in stone, bronze, gold, silver and precious stones. They thus became great storehouses of wealth; so much so that when the Islamic armies started invading Northern India, their attention for plunder was almost solely directed at the temples, which had more treasures than the palaces. Hence, most of the priceless objects which they housed have almost completely disappeared.

Perhaps the flower of Eastern Indian art was to bloom under the great Pala rulers of Bengal. During this period the arts flourished, liberal patronage being given by the Pala rulers, who raised temples and commissioned great sculptures and paintings. By the 11th century the Islamic armies had broken the organisation of the Hindu states, and by the 12th century the Islamic chiefs had obtained a foothold in India, which they were to retain for over seven centuries.

The Islamic advances had a disastrous effect on the bronze art of Northern and Eastern India. Most of the existing statues were destroyed by the army, who were sworn to wipe out idolatory, and all further bronze art was stifled. The only outlet available to the artist was in making small figures of animals and people, as toys or ornaments. And so the chain of the great Eastern Indian bronze tradition was broken irrevocably.

In Nepal and Tibet, however, the traditions of the Gupta and Pala artists continued, although altered by the codes of Lamaistic Buddhism. Some bronze figures of the Pala period survive but they are mostly small pieces, most of the larger ones having been destroyed.

During the 16th and 17th centuries a more lenient attitude was adopted towards the Hindus by the Mughal rulers, and metal statuary again began to be made, but the grandeur of the earlier tradition had been lost.

The oldest bronzes from the Deccan cannot be dated before the 9th century. Although there are magnificent examples of Deccanese stone sculpture which date to the Andhra dynasty (3rd century B.C. to 3rd century A.D.), no examples of bronze work have been found. There is, however, one exception. A miniature bronze figure of an elephant, with riders, was excavated in 1945 from Brahmapuri, Kolhapur. It is, however, only a fragment, probably a finial of a lamp, but shows a highly developed knowledge of bronze working. It belongs to the Satavahana period, mid 2nd century. There is a similar figure of a lone elephant, part of a toy, in the Barrett Collection, which may date to the same period (see *Oriental Art*, volume 4, No. 3, 1953).

If the bronzes from the Deccan are illusive, so the early history is obscure. The period between the end of the Andhra dynasty in the 3rd century A.D. and the beginning of the Chalukya dynasty in the mid 6th century A.D. is extremely hazy. The Chalukya dynasty was founded by Pulakesin; his son, Pulakesin the Second, had to deal with attacks from the north by King Harsha. After a struggle the river Narbada was finally accepted as a boundary between the territories of the two kings. The Chalukyas were Hindus but they were tolerant to other religious sects. During the period, many great works of art were executed.

In the mid-8th century A.D. a new dynasty gained power—the Rashtrakutas—who remained in power for over 250 years. Unlike the Chalukyas, the Rashtrakutas were Jains and gave liberal patronage to Jainism and its works of art.

The Chalukyas enjoyed a brief return to power in the Southern Deccan, when they overthrew the Rashtrakutas in the 10th century. They had, however, to deal with the northern expansionist movement from the South under the Cholas. During this power contest two feudatory lords of the Chalukyas, Haysala of Mysore and Yadava of Devagiri, became extremely powerful and gained their independence from the Chalukyas. Thereafter the Chalukya dynasty soon broke up and the Deccan passed into the hands of the two new dynasties.

During the period from the 12th to 14th centuries, many wonderful temples and works of art were created but were to

8. Bronze bust of a bodhisattva. Andhra Pradesh, Eastern Chalukya style. About A.D. 700. Ht. 13 cm.

meet the same fate as those of Northern India, when the Islamic armies overran the Deccan, sacking and destroying everything in their path. The two capitals were reduced to heaps of rubble.

Bronze art received the patronage of the Hairda king,

Bittedeba, later known as Vishnu Vardhana, after he had embraced the Vaishnava faith. Few examples of bronze art during this period, however, are known.

When we move on to the far south, things are happier. Due to its geographical location, many of the earlier bronzes were

9. Image of a Jina. Jain. From Western India. 9th–10th century.

spared the attention of the Islamic armies. However, it is still difficult to date many of the earliest figures before the 9th century.

The earliest examples of bronze statuary belong to the Chola period. The bronzes show a high technical and artistic skill, suggesting a continuous development of the bronze art of the earlier periods.

The Cholas were warlike kings and during their dynasty they conquered large areas, both in India and abroad. Their fleets sailed across the Bay of Bengal and the Indian Ocean. Ceylon, and many islands of the South fell under their domination. In the mid 10th century they also tried to push northwards and clashed with the Chalukya of the Deccan. After a prolonged struggle they were defeated.

Like many warlike peoples they were patrons of the arts. They built large temples and palaces and commissioned numerous sculptures in metal and stone. During the reign of Kulotunga Chola in the 11th century, many fine bronze sculptures were cast. A number of these masterpieces are known today and provide us with some of the finest examples of Indian metal sculpture. Bronzes from this period are widely sought after and many museums throughout the world have excellent examples.

Art declined in the 13th century, with the downfall of the Cholas, but regained its former splendour for a short time under the powerful Hindu kings of Vijayanagar. The history of Vijayanagar is tragic but interesting. It was founded in the 14th century after a Moslem state revolted and threw off the domination of the Sultan from the north. The state split into independent kingdoms.

Five Hindu brothers formed the Hindu state of Vijayanagar. Although it was constantly at war with its Moslem neighbours it flourished until it was destroyed in 1565.

During the period from its inception until it was finally destroyed, art ran riot. Liberal patronage was given to the arts, and sculpture, architecture and painting flourished. A very fine figure of King Krishna Deva Raja and his two queens is in the Museum of Fine Arts, Boston. The figures show another skill of the bronze worker—repoussé. The figures, 59 cm. high, are beautifully made in beaten copper.

Although bronze casting continued in the far South, un-broken by the Moslem intrusion, it gradually degenerated. The figures of the 19th century are mere echoes of a once majestic art. There are, however, exceptions and within the

Colour Plate
3. A very fine gilt bronze figure of Sadaksari–Lokesvara. Tibet. 18th century. Ht. 13 cm.

10. Bronze figure of Manjusri. Javanese. 10th century A.D. Ht. 15 cm.

framework of each century and period one can find bronzes worth collecting; masterpieces of their period.

As mentioned earlier, Indian bronzes vary considerably in composition, pure copper, brass and bronze being used. Gold, silver and alloys, such as Astadhatu, were also used. Astadhatu, an alloy of eight different metals—gold, silver, iron, lead, tin, copper, zinc and mercury—principally used in Northern India, was considered very precious for making religious figures. The equivalent South Indian alloy was the Pancha Lauha, an alloy made from five metals: copper, gold, silver, brass and lead (brass, in this case, being treated as a pure metal).

The cire perdue, or lost wax method of casting, allows the artist great freedom and enables him to produce many intricate designs. The image was first sculpted in bees-wax, preferably of a light yellow colour to simulate the colour of the metal in which it was to be cast, thus ensuring that the artist had the same lighting effect on his original model as that on the finished bronze.

Colour Plate
4. Tibetan bronze figure of the Buddha. 18th century. Ht. 16 cm.

33

11. Bronze figure of Durga killing the demon Mahishasura. 18th century. South-west India. Ht. 13 cm.

The wax original was then covered with a layer of fine clay. Charred husk, minced cotton, salt and other ingredients were mixed with the clay. The image was covered with three layers, holes being left in the casing for the wax to escape and to allow the molten metal to be introduced. A final, thicker layer covered the whole. The image was then placed in a fire or oven until most of the wax had melted and evaporated away and until only the composition mould was left. The molten metal was then poured into the mould and left until cool. The mould was then broken open to reveal a metal copy of the original wax sculpture. Variations of this method were used at different

12. Bronze figure of Krishna playing the flute (missing). East India. 19th century. Note traces of pigment still adhering to the figure. Precise dating of these figures is very difficult, it may be earlier. Ht. 25 cm.

periods and are still used in India today.

An interesting example of casting technique used to make the large bronze figures of the Gupta period can be seen by examining the great figure of Buddha from Sultangunj in the

Birmingham Museum. The figure was cast in copper in two layers on to a core composed of a mixture of clay, sand, charcoal and rice husks. The first layer was moulded directly to the core and was hèld together by iron bands. The outer surface was then probably cast over the first layer by the cire perdue method. The whole image seems to have been made in different sections.

13. Indian bronze image of Vishnu with attendants. Of the Pala period of Bengal. 10th century A.D. Note features worn down due to constant handling.

The village craftsmen sometimes used a different method of making their bronzes, using strips of metal which were bound together around a composition core.

How to Identify Indian Bronzes

Probably most important to collectors is to know what the bronze is, what date it is and where it comes from. There are numerous deities in India, all religions, except the Mohammedan, producing bronze images. Reference to the glossary on iconography and to the identification charts of poses and mudras will help with the identification of the figure—though be warned: there are many unusual images, often from villages, that do not fit into the codes of the classical schools. These are usually village gods and unless one is extremely lucky they are likely to remain unidentified.

Dating Indian bronzes is much more difficult. In the beginning the collector will not find it easy. There are so many different factors that one must appreciate when appraising a piece. It is essential not only to have a good knowledge of the main schools of Indian art but to be familiar with the differences of the various periods and places. The figure must be examined very carefully, taking note of the subject, the quality of the modelling, the casting, the finishing of the surface and the general condition of the bronze, both on the surface and on the base. Also, note should be taken of the costumes prevalent in India at the different places and periods, some deities and poses being more popular in some regions than others. Often, identification of the subject will help considerably. Finally, images of some gods may only have been made in certain periods.

There are several ways in which the collector can familiarise himself with the different schools and learn to identify the bronzes. Books, visits to museums and personal handling are all important. There are many specialised books on the subject (see bibliography) — but, beware, books alone are not sufficient. Without seeing and handling specimens one can often reach the wrong conclusion. Visits must be made to as many museums as possible which have good collections of oriental art. Try, whenever possible, to handle bronzes. This not only gives one a closer look but also alerts the other senses. Soon you will find that you are able to tell things which are impossible to describe in a book. If you handle sufficient bronzes your mind subconsciously makes notes of such things as weight, feel of the contours, etc., and these are all very important when assessing an unfamiliar piece.

Good opportunities to handle bronzes and to buy occur at the principal sale rooms, where specialist sales are held. Here, one is also aided by a catalogue and one can play a guessing game, personally assess the piece, and then check with the catalogue. Do not be surprised, however, if you are wrong, there is much to learn. Even some attributions included in such catalogues can be wrong and another important factor is that two experts can give different attributions to the same piece. Finally, remember that most museums containing oriental collections will be pleased to help with attributions.

The Gupta period produced the first important styles in Indian metal sculpture. A study of the stone sculptures of the period will often help in understanding the various stylistic differences. The human figures and anthromorphic figures of the gods are sculptured with slim bodies. The limbs have been beautifully modelled. The face often has smooth serene features and one can see the strong influence of the placid doctrines of Buddhism.

The hair of Gupta images is often extremely stylised and formal. The coiffure of the Buddha images is shown as snail-shell curls. The robes are shown as mere suggestions, clinging to the body, revealing the beautifully proportioned slim figure of the deity. As mentioned earlier, the majority of the images of the period have been destroyed, with one or two notable exceptions. Bronzes of this period are, therefore, very rare and the collector is unlikely to find examples.

In Eastern India, Bengal and Bihar, the Pala school was also Buddhistic and the images show the artistic ideals of Buddhism, at the same time being influenced by an earlier period of post-Gupta rise in the Brahmanic faith. This is sometimes revealed by the fact that some Pala Buddhist images are mixed with Hindu iconography. Although the Pala dynasty was Buddhist, many Hindu images were also made.

Pala artists continued to model figures with slim bodies but the robe was shown as a simple suggestion, the figures being naked above the waist. Jewellery was shown and became extremely elaborate during the late Pala period. Facial features became very sharp and aquiline. Most large bronzes of the period have been lost, destroyed by the invading Moslem armies, but it is possible to obtain small bronzes which, in many cases, are miniature masterpieces of the period. Some have been preserved simply by the fact of their small size. They were either used as personal images and kept about the person, or the larger ones kept in personal altars in the house. Others were preserved when they were lost or buried and these often have a pleasing patina.

Apart from the bronzes in the traditional classical style, there are others in a provincial style.

Bronzes contemporary with the Pala school were made in other parts of Northern India, especially at Malwa. These are mainly small pieces and are similar to the Pala style, though retaining their provincial character. Bronzes from this period are often made easier to date by inscriptions. This is also true of the bronzes from the Deccan, especially figures of Jain Tirthankaras of the 13th to 14th century. Examples of the earlier art of the Deccan are very rare. Some bronze figures

14. Extremely fine bronze figure of Durga. From Nalanda, Pala. 10th century A.D. Ht. 9·5 cm.

which date to the 3rd century were found at Amaravati but otherwise we have virtually nothing to go on, except the stone sculpture. The western Chalukya sculpture shows strong Gupta influence but there are no bronze examples.

The southern sculpture of the Tamils was strongly influenced by the sculptural styles of Amaravati. The earlier bronze figures are generally ascribed to the Chola period, though some experts would date them to the earlier Pallava dynasty.

Perhaps the greatest number of Indian images came from Southern India. The Chola period produced fine examples of deities in vigorous postures, a notable example being the numerous figures of Siva Nataraja—Siva as Lord of the Dance. A large number of the Chola sculptures show various forms of Siva, sometimes alone and at other times with his wife, Parvati,

15. Back view of Pala bronze figure. No. 14.

and his son, Skanda. Other images are shown more serene.
Figures of kings and queens are known, executed singly and in
groups. Another form of sculpture very popular during the
Chola period is the Dipa Lakshmi, sometimes known as
'beauty-lights'. These are female figures holding a lamp;
sometimes the figure modelled on the donor. These figures may
have been used either for the Arati ceremony or for burning
lights at night in front of the deities, symbolising the eternal
devotion of the donor. Many Chola bronzes, both Dipa Lakshmi and other figures, are inscribed with a short dedication
and the name of the donor.

16. Small bronze image of Siva seated with his consort Parvati on his knee. Malwa. 10th–11th century A.D. Ht. 7 cm.

17. Bronze figure of Siva and his consort, Uma. Madras state. Chola style. About A.D. 1000 Ht. 46 cm.

The sculptural superiority of the Chola figure is easy to see. The body is beautifully modelled, full advantage being taken of the vitality of the human body. In the early Chola period, the figures, although formalised to a certain extent, are more realistic than those of the later period. The breasts of female figures are prominent, round and sculptured with sympathy. The faces are smooth and round, with simple features. Most wear clothing only from the waist downwards. Jewellery is simple and used to great effect. Necklaces hang down in circles and, on female figures, hang between the breasts. A bangle is usually shown worn above the elbow.

The facial features of the late Chola period become stiffer, the nose more prominent and the torso thicker and stiffer.

Ceylon

Before leaving the subject of South Indian bronzes it is necessary to consider the wonderful examples of metal sculpture of Ceylon, which must be studied together with those of South India. The influence of the Pallava and Chola artists was very strong in Ceylon, local schools producing figures in their styles. Although many beautiful examples have survived, most of the very early pieces, before the 8th or 9th century, are missing.

Some of the bronzes found in Ceylon are so similar to the South Indian that they may well have been cast there. Others are different in a way that is Singhalese. Only comparison between the South Indian art forms will show the subtle differences inherent in the Singhalese images. As in India, certain icons are more popular than others. Pattini Deva was one of the favoured goddesses. A beautiful image of her was found on the north-eastern coast between Trincomalee and Ballicalwa. Of uncertain age, it shows all the artistic traits of the Gupta sculpture of Northern India of the 5th century, though this is, perhaps, a coincidence and should not be taken as an indication of age. It must also be admitted that it is very

18. Miniature gilt bronze image of the Buddha seated in the dhyan asana and in the dhyana mudra. Note flame usnisa. South India. 16th century. Ht. 6·5 cm.

similar to the figures of the apsaras of the Sigiriya frescoes, and, if one takes this as a valid comparison, may date from the 6th to the 8th century.

Fine bronzes of the 10th century have been found near the ancient capital of Anuradhapura. A miniature pair of feet in bronze show the same casting technique as the Sultangunj

43

19. Tara of Pappini Deva. This piece is given different dates by different authorities. It shows artistic traits of the Gupta sculpture of Northern India of the 5th century, and also to the Sigiriya frescoes, which if a valid comparison may date to the 6th–8th century A.D. The British Museum prefer to date the sculpture to the 10th-11th century A.D. Ht. 143 cm.

Buddha but have iron as a core.

An extremely interesting group of bronzes, probably dating from the 12th to 13th century, were found at Polonnaruwa in 1906. They are very large, and though some experts maintain that they are Singhalese, others, like Vincent Smith, maintain that they were imported from the mainland. There are some very fine miniature bronzes in various museums and it is possible to find good examples on the open market.

So far, I have concentrated on describing bronzes of the principal classical schools of Indian art, mainly of an early date. It is important to know these because it is possible, on rare occasions, to find examples in antique shops or showrooms. One can, of course, purchase from specialists but the price will be appropriate to the rarity of the item.

Collecting Indian bronzes, however, is a fascinating hobby, because there are many fine examples of bronzes (mainly small), of periods dating from the 10th century, that can be collected. An unfortunate myth perpetrated in the past was that bronzes dating after the medieval period were not worth collecting. This, of course, is not the case. There are good and bad examples from all periods. In order to help with the dating of these later bronzes it will be necessary to see something of the later schools and village work.

Folk or Jungli Bronzes
Folk bronzes have been made at all periods, along with those

20. Miniature bronze figure of Hanuman. This little figure has the movement and power of a much larger sculpture. Deccan. 17th century. Ht. 8 cm.

belonging more to the classical schools, but whereas the classical pieces have survived in temples and families, the folk variety are rare before the 16th to 17th century, mainly due to their rural environment. Dedicated to village deities, they were often replaced, either with new images of the same god or with new gods, when dedications changed. Another cause is that villages are rarely excavated, so many of the earlier examples lie hidden from modern eyes beneath centuries of debris.

Unlike the bronzes of the classical schools, the Jungli bronze

21. Fine bronze image of Parvati. An excellent example of good quality later bronze casting. Note the chasing and ornamentation. South India. 18th–19th century. Ht. 20 cm.

is the work of local village craftsmen, and is therefore not influenced by the canons of Sanskrit literature, which laid down the bodily proportions of the deities. The village artist used a skill and tradition unchanged for centuries, passed down to him from father to son. Not only was he free from the rigid canons which governed the classical school but he also used different techniques in modelling and casting, albeit cruder

22. An Eastern Indian Jungli bronze figure of a calf. 18th–19th century. Ht. 5 cm.

than the classical school, but often resulting in extremely pleasing, vigorous works. He also had the advantage of portraying new and original village gods and saints, together with those of the orthodox Vedic group, which were popular in villages.

These bronzes show the human figure greatly simplified. They often appear to be very crude examples of the Pala period, or bad copies. Many of the features found on Pala images can also be seen on the Jungli. The stands are often oblong; sometimes open-worked, and sometimes with legs. The method of attaching the aureole to the figure is reminiscent of Pala work. It often has a diamond open-work, or solid zig-zag flame surround. As in Pala pieces, groups are more common

47

than single figures. Although probably retaining some small influence from the early period, the Jungli can in no way compare with the Pala pieces, either in modelling or casting, and the comparison is, therefore, only meant as a reflection.

Because of the conservatism of village craftsmen, it is often very difficult to date Jungli pieces. It would not be surprising for virtually no change to have been made in the modelling technique for a thousand years or more, and it is still possible to obtain figures made this century identical with those of the 17th century. Superficially the general appearance of this class of bronze is very similar to figures made in Luristan in Persia from the 8th to 10th century B.C.

The modelling of Jungli pieces is often extremely crude, but pleasing. The metal seems to take on the plasticity of the wax original. Cast in bronze or brass, the main details were often

23. Bronze figure of Garuda, finial of utensil. 18th–19th century. Central India. Ht. 8 cm.

added later by engraving. The cire perdue method was used for casting but often the wax original was modelled on a core of composition or mortar, which was removed after casting, though in many cases was left. The cast was finally filed and

Colour Plate
5. A fine pair of bronze figures of Radha and Krishna. Krishna in the Venugopala pose. Bengal. 18th century. Ht. 15 cm and 12 cm.

24. An unusual bronze figure of Siva dn Parvati, joined together on common base. The workmanship is typical Jungli but very archaic. 17th century. Ht. 9 cm.

Colour Plate
6. An octagonal copper gilt box in repoussé, decorated with flora and fauna and with a central panel depicting a deity in tantric manifestation. 18th–19th century. Nepal. Ht. 4·5 cm.

smoothed, and often painted. Some figures have traces of paint still adhering, sometimes with additional traces of vermilion placed on the figure during worshipping.

It is not uncommon for Jungli figures to be confused with

25. Jungli figure of Siva with Parvati, part of a larger figure group. 19th century. Ht. 10 cm.

castings of the classical school, made in the mid- and late 19th century, from Eastern India, especially Bengal, which have painted features superficially similar to the Jungli, but, on closer examination, quite different. Many pieces give the impression of being built up with lattice-work and coilings.

The face of the Jungli is highly stylised, with sharp features, sometimes bizarre, or even grotesque. The eyes are modelled in the shape of almonds, with lids applied as strip surrounds. The nose is protruding, often aquiline. With figures of Ganesha, the trunk is often shown long and thin. Limbs are modelled extremely fluidly, with little or no definition between the anatomical sections. Most figures are shown with headresses

26. Jungli bronze figure seated on a lotus base and holding lotuses in each ahdn and surrounded by a flame aureole. Probably Surya. 18th century. Ht. 14 cm.

which are either conical or in the shape of an elaborate crown.

Female figures are shown with breasts built up as coils or looped as a horizontal figure of 8. Animals are mostly modelled on a core, with lattice-work; sometimes with legs constructed as coils.

Subjects vary according to region and period but the most common seem to have been representations of the deities, Durga, Siva, the Lingam, Ganesha, Annapurna, Krishna, the Nandi Bull and Naga, Vishnu, Khandarao, Lakshmi, and Durga as Mahishasura-Mardini. These are mostly found as group figures, though they also occur singly or in pairs, especially Krishna, Durga and Siva.

27. Bronze vermilion holder and two mango 'purses'. Eastern India. 18th century.

A common feature to most groups is the Lingam. One such group from Central India may, for example, show Khandarao, an aspect of Siva, on horseback, carrying a sword and shield, and an attendant figure behind him, with the figure of Annapurna on the right corner and the Lingam on the left.

Apart from the popular gods of the Hindu Pantheon, figures of local gods, agricultural and original deities and saints were

52

also made. This type of figure is virtually impossible to identify.

Besides figures, other objects were also made by the same craftsmen and were executed in a similar fashion. Still with religious connections, were toys, such as elephants and horses

28. Jungli bronze elephant lamp with female rider. 19th century.

on wheels, surmounted with a figure or group of figures of deities. These can be recognised as distinct from pure toys. Many of the gods were represented on animals, such as the elephant, the horse and even the peacock. These wheeled figures or toys are very similar in idea to the terracottas dating to the 2nd and 3rd centuries B.C., which have been unearthed at sites such as Tamralipta or Tamluk, and Berachampa in the Twenty-Four Parganas near Calcutta. These figures were either made in the form of the animal Vahana of the gods, or as groups, with the deity surmounting the animal. It is thought that these were used by children in religious ceremonies in much the same way as children in the West play with crib models, etc., at Christmas. The bronze worker did not restrict himself, however, to the purely religious, for he made lamps, pan and spice boxes, purses, vermilion holders and many other objects of utility, but still using the same techniques as he used on the figures. Some of these objects are made in the form

29. Jungli bronze figure of a peacock with god rider. Probably Subrahmanya. 19th century. This figure formerly had wheels attached and was pulled along as a toy. Ht. 20 cm.

of birds, fish and, sometimes, fruit, such as the mango.

Collecting Jungli pieces can be extremely rewarding, often enabling the collector to acquire original, spontaneous works of art, which are sometimes lacking in the classical school.

Later Bronze Art

Before we go on to consider the bronze statuary of Tibet and Nepal we should pay some attention to the bronze work of the later periods of the mainstream of Indian art. Although the same greatness was never achieved again after the golden ages of the medieval period, many fine works were produced and deserve attention.

After the Islamic invasion, when so many of India's bronze masterpieces were destroyed, it was impossible for the bronze worker to work on images in safety. He therefore directed his attention to the production of utilitarian objects until such time, generations later, when the age-old craft could be continued. By this time the deft touch of the old masters had vanished. Their descendants did not know the little tricks and skills that their ancestors had employed. Many started with little or no experience of figure modelling, save for work on toys, etc., while others chose to ignore the freer atmosphere and continued to make toys and other objects.

The artists had lost their touch—but not for long, and within the confines of their new environment and social conditions, bronzes were again made for personal shrines and for the adornment of temples, but time had left its mark, clearly recognisable on the metal art. Many of the figures seemed to be poor copies of earlier pieces, or had a modern element, combined with some of the techniques used in the production of toys and utilitarian pieces.

The bronzes of South India during the 17th, 18th and 19th centuries became stiff and formalised and, to a certain extent, stylised. They lost much of their original plasticity. The metal art of the Deccan was similarly affected, though here many toy-like and folk features slipped into the art. Rajasthan and Central India were no exception. Bihar, Orissa and Bengal were more fluid in style, though often the figures were thickly modelled, with sharp features, the details being engraved after casting.

Although, on the face of it, these figures seem poor substitutes for the earlier pieces, many original and interesting icons were produced which are well worth collecting. They retain some of the earlier qualities, while expressing them in an original way.

30. A Deccan saivite bronze image. 18th century. Ht. 10 cm.

The surface of many of these bronzes is unfinished and very rough, due to the fact that they were often painted, especially those from Bengal.

During the later periods there were large numbers of figures made of the popular gods in the regions. In South India, Vishnu

31. Bronze image of Vishnu, in three parts. South India. 18th–19th century. Ht. 18 cm.

was very popular, and there are numerous images, modelled in three parts: the figure, the square base, and the prabha or aureole, these being slotted together to form a composite piece. Vishnu was usually shown in a stiff, stylised attitude, with four arms, holding the usual attributes, while the prabha was portrayed as a flame aura, with a Naga canopy above his head. A popular group sculpture was Somaskanda, which showed Uma and Siva, with their son Skanda. Various representations of the god Siva, some as Nataraja—Lord of the Dance—and some with his consort Parvati, as well as figures of Parvati alone, were also popular.

57

32. Small copper figure of Lakshmi. 18th century. 4¼ in. South India. Ht. 11 cm.

The Lingam was also constantly represented, as were various
Saivite saints and local heroes. In the Deccan, Jain figures of
Mahavira were popular. Dipa Lakshmis were made in South
India, the Deccan (some in Central India) and Eastern India,
especially Bengal. Figures of Krishna, with the milkmaid
Radha, were very popular in Eastern India—Bengal, Orissa
and Bihar—while figures of Ganesha were produced over most
of India. Durga was a popular deity in the east.

In Eastern India, Krishna (Venugopala) was portrayed
playing the flute to Radha, and as a baby, on all fours, playing
with a pat of butter. In South India a popular representation

of Krishna was the Navanita-Niritta-Murti, showing Krishna as a dancing boy. Images of Krishna portray him in various moods, reflecting his upbringing among the cowherds. He was a mischievous child and was always playing jokes on the milk-maids. The representations of Krishna in Eastern India,

33. A bronze figure of Krishna in the Venugopala pose playing on his flute to Radha. The figure has a fine patina and originally had silver eyes. Bengal 18th century. Ht. 14 cm.

showing him on all fours, with a pat of butter, and in South India, dancing with a pat of butter, portray an episode in his life as a child, when he stole a ball of butter from the milk churn when his step-mother was not looking, and danced for joy.

59

34. A bronze figure of Radha, companion figure to plate 33. Bengal 18th century. Ht. 14 cm.

TIBETAN AND NEPALESE METAL ART

Tibet, the roof of the world, is a cold land. Most of it lies at an altitude of between 10,000 and 20,000 feet above sea level, covering an area of, possibly, 700,000 square miles. The winds are sharp and terrible, blowing from about eleven in the morning till after sunset. It is a dry land, with only about eight inches of rain a year on the Tibetan uplands.

The Tibetans are related to the Mongolians, and, like them, many are nomads. The early settlers of Nepal probably came from Tibet, and the people of Bhutan, Sikkim and Ladakh are also of Mongolian stock.

The Tibetans' diet is an austere one, with few luxuries. They are fond of meat, though a substantial part of the diet is barley.

35. Painted figure of Bala–Krishna. Bengal. 18th century. Ht. 8 cm.

The common dish is Tsam-pa—barley flour. Barley is also used to make beer, which must be freshly made and is drunk from special containers with a straw or tube. Children are not weaned from their mothers until they are two, or even three years old, and this practice is thought to act as a primitive form of birth control, and although the land is poor, there is sufficient food for all.

The early bronze art of Nepal and Tibet, which must include border states, such as Bhutan, Sikkim and Ladakh, was strongly influenced by the classical schools of the Gupta and Pala periods. In Nepal the sculpture of the 7th and 8th centuries A.D. shows a very strong influence of the Gupta art, and the figures look pure Indian in character, with no trace of Mongolian features showing in the modelling. They are as near as possible to Taranatha's 'School of the East', and according to some authorities may bear some relation to the later Pala schools of Dhiman and Bitpalo.

Indian sculpture itself was imported into Nepal during the Gupta period and thence to Tibet. Nepalese art shows an almost unbroken continuity from the earliest times, unaffected by the Islamic invasions which had such a disastrous effect upon the bronze art of other parts of India. The earliest pieces show a very strong affinity to the sculpture of Eastern India, especially Bengal.

As mentioned previously, the early Nepalese images are

36. Bronze figure of Radha. Bengal. 18th–19th century. Ht. 23 cm.

almost entirely Indian in character. They are full-bodied and the face is shown with a rounded nose and full lips, which contrast with those of later dates, when the face became narrower, the lips thinner in outline and the nose aquiline. This is especially noticeable in bronzes from about the 15th century onwards.

During the later periods there was a marked increase in the decoration of the figures, which were often studded with semi-precious stones. Numerous bangles, anklets and necklaces were cast on to the figures, which were adorned with elaborate headresses and garments, with chased designs. The hands, too, became extremely slender. As time progressed from the 10th century, the Mongolian features gradually became more and more pronounced, until many of the later figures show eyes as mere slits.

The iconography of the Nepalese pieces is Buddhist but with strong overtones from Hindu India. The iconography, too, becomes more and more complicated in the later periods.

Tibetan images, like the early Nepalese, were strongly influenced by early Indian originals, and retain a great deal of the early Indian style even to the present day. In Tibet, the influences were more complex. In addition to those from India and Nepal, the sculpture was affected by the Buddhist images of China, which themselves were influenced by the Gupta and Greco-Indian schools of sculpture. So we have, in effect, direct influence from India on the one hand and indirect—coloured by Chinese thought—on the other. We know from manuscripts that there were Indian artists who worked in China. A Chinese transcription mentions the name of Ar Ni Ko, a Nepalese artist, painter, sculptor and decorator, who was invited, in the 13th century, to the court of the Chinese Emperor. He wrote 'A Canon of Proportions', which was translated into Chinese in the 17th century, and in 1885 was printed in Japan.

The imagery of Nepal and Tibet is extremely complicated, the number of icons is infinite, and to appreciate, fully, Tibetan and Nepalese art, much attention should be paid to the study of the iconography of Tibetan Lamaism.

There is one major difference in the technique used by the Tibetan and Nepalese artists, as compared with the Indian. A school of repoussé work (i.e., the construction of images in beaten sheet metal, hammered into shape from the reverse side) grew up alongside the traditional technique of bronze casting by the cire perdue method. Many of the larger pieces were constructed in this manner, being made in separate sections and then joined together. It was, perhaps, the amalgamation of the artist's and bronze caster's techniques with those of the copper and goldsmith. The same craftsmen often produced reliquaries and god boxes, etc., and many other religious objects, with relief decorations executed by repoussé.

Many of the images were gilded and coloured; in some cases only the face, and in others the whole image. The eyes and nose were often painted and the hair coloured blue, a sign of

37. Gilt bronze figure of Tara. Nepalese. 14th century A.D. or earlier. Ht. 26 cm.

holiness. Some of the larger images were actually clothed.

A unique feature of Tibetan and Nepalese bronzes is that in the majority of cases they were cast hollow, and the inside sealed with prayers and offerings, which, among other things,

Colour Plate

7. An unusual copper gilt phurbu in the form of a diety wearing dharmapala ornaments. Probably Acaryavajrapani. Tibet. 18th century. Ht. 16·5 cm.

included grain and even precious stones. Sometimes a miniature icon was also included. All this was sealed with a copper sheet, bearing the sign of crossed Vajras, which sometimes also bore an inscription. Collectors should never remove this base without proper advice from authorities, as in many cases valuable information is contained therein, sometimes including the date of dedication. The base can be removed but it must be done in a way which will not spoil the image and which will enable the seal to be replaced. The sealing of these images was usually done in the presence of monks and lamas in temples.

Prior to the introduction of Buddhism, the Tibetans were followers of Bonpo or Pon, a religion which combined elements of sorcery and sexual mysticism, and practised human and animal sacrifices. Legend has it that it was the Chinese and Nepalese wives of the Tibetan king Srong-san-gan-po who first introduced Buddhism into Tibet in the 7th century A.D. Both were devout Buddhists and brought with them sacred images. They are also credited with introducing the alphabet, which was adapted from an Indian prototype, brought by Indian Buddhist teachers who had been sent for by the wives. This was used in making translations of the sacred books.

The conversion of the population to Buddhism was slow before the 8th century A.D. The old religion, which was greatly feared, had a strong hold on the people. In A.D. 747 a Tibetan king named Ti-song-de-tsen sent to a monastery at Nalanda in Bihar for Padmasambhava, a famous teacher of Tantric Buddhism, to come to Tibet to help convert the populace. He brought with him a form of Tantric Buddhism to which he added elements and deities of Pon. The result is what we know today as Lamaism.

The word 'Lama' was derived from the Tibetan 'Bla-ma', meaning 'superior one'. It is also applied to religious teachers and to the heads of monasteries. Padmasambhava is known in Tibet as Guru-rin-pocche, founder of Lamaism and generally thought of as a saint. He founded the Red Cap Sect or Nying-ma-pa.

Tantric Buddhism was best suited to Tibet, as it was more akin to the old religion. In India it was added to the doctrine of Mahayana in the 6th century A.D. The Tantric doctrine is the worship of the Sakti, or energy of the god, usually expressed as female, in conjunction with the male force.

Saktis of the Bodhisattvas are depicted as icons of Taras. Tantric images are shown either pacific or angry, with multiple heads or arms, and sometimes both. The name comes from the

Colour Plate
8. A Jungli bronze figure of an elephant. The central spike was made to take a god rider. Eastern India. 18th century. Ht. 9 cm.

65

Tantras (treatise) on the worship of the Sakti and the attainment of Perfection or the Eight Siddhis.

India, too, at this time was much affected by primitive ideas of magic and sexual mysticism and in the 8th century 'The Vehicle of the Thunderbolt', the Vajrayana, a combination of primitive cults and Buddhism, grew up in Eastern India. It was introduced into Japan at an early date and still survives there as the Shingon Sect. In the 11th century it was established in Tibet by Atisa and missionaries from the Vajrayana monastery of Vikramasila in Bihar. Atisa, a Hindu priest, founded the Ka-dam-pa Sect in 1040. This was later reformed by the teacher Tsong-k-a-pa to become the premier sect of Tibet, the Yellow Cap Sect or Ge-lug-pa.

Another sect formed in the 11th century was Kar-gyu-pa, founded by Mar-pa, a disciple of Atisa.

Alongside these there still exist Ponist monasteries; the White Pon, which is similar to Buddhism but which has deities that differ as to attributes and names, and priests of the Black Hats or Black Pon, who are greatly feared by the people as sorcerers.

The life of Tibet is dominated by religion. Over a third of the population, prior to the Chinese invasion, were monks. The Tibetan religious system is graded, and the majority belong to the lowest grade, the Ge-long, having obtained the grade by serving as novices (Ge-tshul) and attendants (Ge-nyen).

Most families supplied at least one male member, who was taken to the monastery when still a child. Only a small proportion of women, however, became nuns. The Ge-long lived in monasteries and officiated at routine rites. The abbots were known as Khan-po, while the highest grade, the Avatara Lamas, were divided into classes.

Thought to be incarnations, the Tul-ku were incarnations of saints—either Tibetan or Indian—and the Khuluktu were incarnations of deities. The highest of these is the Dalai Lama, the spiritual and temporal head of Tibet and the incarnation of Bodhisattva Avalokitesvara. The Panchen Lama is the incarnation of Amitabha Buddha.

There are over 300 divinities of the Ge-lug-pa (Yellow Cap) sect, of which there are numerous variations. For example, Bhattacharya, an Indian historian says there are over 108 forms of Avalokitesvara. To this must be added the deities and infinite variations of the other sects, and of Pon. It will be clear from this that identification of Tibetan icons can be extremely difficult, unless they are of the more common variety.

38. Lid, part of large bronze censer. Nepal. 17th century or earlier. The motif is interesting depicting, monkeys, geese and mongooses. Ht. 10·5 cm.

Identification of an image starts with noting all the details: the ornaments, clothes, mudras and asanas, the vahanas and attributes. Reference to the glossaries and charts at the back of the book will help in this respect.

The images, together with Thang-kas and other paraphernalia, were an important part of the religion, which was dominated by ritual and magic. In a religion such as this, no allowance could be made for variations, so there were rigid canons which determined the image's features and proportions,

39. Gilt bronze figure of Lokesvara, with Diminutive Buddha headdress. Nepal/Bihar border.
17th century. Ht. 16 cm.

etc. As a discipline, however, it allowed the individual creative
power of the artist, usually a member of the priesthood,
freedom of expression within the discipline. This often resulted

40. Bronze figure of the goddess Ganga standing on Makara. The figure shows traces of painting. Nepal. 19th century. Ht. 19 cm.

in works of art and an image worthy of worship. Many are works of individual genius, the result of inspiration through meditation. Most of the art of Tibet was made for religious purposes and a large proportion of this for the instruction of religious teachings. The Thang-kas (banner paintings) are probably the best examples of this.

Apart from images made for the adornment of temples, special rooms were kept in some for storing icons. They were also made for private shrines and for carrying on the person in god boxes. Travelling monks also kept images in small portable shrines.

Buddhism in Nepal was introduced at an earlier date than in Tibet. The Buddha himself was born not far from the borders of Nepal, and legend has it that he visited the land himself. The oldest Buddhist monuments in Nepal are thought to be Mauryan in origin and it is not impossible for the Emperor, Asoka, to have been to Nepal himself.

Bronze figures of the early periods are rare, though there are some fine examples in the Boston Museum of Fine Arts, and an extremely interesting one in the British Museum, London. The Padmapani in the Boston collection recalls the elegance of the Bodhisattvas of the Pala period of Eastern India. The drapery style is archaic, having originally been derived from the late Buddhist figures of Gandhara. This is found on early Buddhist sculptures in China and Central Asia, and it is still noticeable on Tibetan images today.

The appearance and ornamentation of Tibetan icons can be divided into six groups: those dressed in Bodhisattva ornaments, Dharmapala ornaments, monastic costumes and miscellaneous garments; nude figures and animal and non-human manifestations.

Bodhisattva ornaments and costumes are worn by mild manifestations, while the Dharmapala costumes are worn by angry or fierce manifestations. Both include Tantric and non-Tantric forms and Yab-yum. The Dharmapala ornaments are reserved for angry manifestations, represented, usually, by a human-type face with angry expression; and fierce manifestations, shown with monstrous features, usually with fangs. Some deities are made with either Bodhisattva or Dharmapala ornaments, and some with both. Yab-yum figures are always Tantric and both Bodhisattva and Dharmapala ornaments are princely.

Icons with Bodhisattva ornaments wear ear-rings, necklaces, armlets, bracelets, wristlets and anklets; a shawl over the

70

41. Tibetan bronze figure of Tara, seated in lalitsana. 18th century. Ht. 13 cm.

42. Tibetan gilt bronze figure of Avalokitesvara. Originally jewelled. Ht. 19 cm.

lower limbs; a five-leaf crown; garlands to the thighs and navel; and a scarf, a girdle and a sash.

Dharmapala ornaments are meant to terrify. The crown is made of five skulls, the garlands and belts are of skulls, and there is sometimes an apron of human bones. Necklaces, anklets and wristlets, etc., are sometimes shown as snakes. Dharmapala icons have the urna. The manifestation usually has the hair arranged in a flame aureole and wears an elephant or tiger-skin on some part of the body.

Manifestations in monastic garments have peaked caps, with long lappets over the ears, and do not wear ornaments.

A shawl is sometimes draped over the shoulder.

43. A bronze Vaishnavite image of tantric manifestations. Bihar. 18th century. Ht. 13 cm.

Icons in other garments include those dressed in Tibetan costume, with broad-brimmed hats; Indian costume, with turbans; and warriors' costume, carrying weapons.

A list of images which wear the different costumes and ornaments is given in the gods and mythology glossary at the back of the book.

As mentioned earlier, there are numerous icons, representing the various deities in different poses and forms. However, at certain periods, and at certain places, there have been favourite gods to depict, and the collector is fortunate in this respect, that in the beginning he will find he is acquiring most of the common forms. The numerous variations are very much rarer, and

44. A Tibetan bronze censer in the form of a deity wearing dharmapala ornaments. 19th century. Ht. 16 cm.

usually good examples of their kind are very much sought after. The more common icons depict Buddha, the Bodhisattvas, the Taras and historical personages, such as Padmasambhava, Srong san gan po, etc.

Although it is encouraging to note that there are common deities, they are often represented in uncommon variations, both in the Bodhisattva and Dharmapala ornaments, and are

45. Large bronze figure of Ganesha (Ganpati), seated on a coiled serpent. Nepal. 18th–19th century. Part of extremely large composite group. Free standing relief. Ht. 43 cm.

shown in both their Tantric and non-Tantric forms.

There are several manifestations of the Adibuddha or primordial Buddha—Creator of the Universe—each one worshipped by a different sect. The Ge-lug-pa (Yellow Cap

46. Copper gilt figure of Amitayus. Tibet. 16th century. Ht. 15 cm.

Sect) worships him as Vajradhara, the Ka-dam-pa (Red Cap Sect) as Vajrasattva and the Nying-ma-pa (unreformed Red Cap Sect) as Samantabhadra. The manifestations of Adi-buddha usuall wear Bodhisattva ornaments and have their

hair done in a high chignon, surmounted by the Cintamani.
They have long-lobed ears and, sometimes, the urna.

47. Miniature image, probably Sitajambhala. Only 2·5 cm high it was sealed inside a larger
icon. 18th century.

Adibuddha as Samantabhadra is usually shown nude,
without ornaments. The spiritual sons of the Adibuddha, the
Dhyanibuddhas, are sometimes called the Five Celestial Jinas.
They, too, usually have long-lobed ears, the usnisa and the
urna. They have no ornaments and wear a monastic shawl over
one shoulder and arm. They can also be shown in Yab-yum,
and, when in this manifestation, wear Bodhisattva ornaments
and garments.

Apart from the Adibuddhas and Dhyanibuddhas, there are
the Manusibuddhas, or mortal Buddhas.

The manifestation of Sakyamuni was the fourth (the present
world cycle), according to the Tri-kaya system.

48. Tibetan bronze figure of Padmasambhava. Founder of Lamaism. 19th century. Ht. 6·5 cm.

49. Gilt bronze figure of Avalokitesvara. Nepalese. 14th century A.D. Ht. 16 cm.

50. Navanita-nritta Krishna. Krishna dancing with a pat of butter. South India. 19th century.
Ht. 12 cm.

Colour Plate
9. Very fine gilt bronze figure of Avalokitesvara. Nepalese. 14th century A.D.
Ht. 16 cm.

The future Buddha, Maitreya, is supposed to appear during the fifth world cycle as the Manusibuddha.

These manifestations are shown with monastic costume, without ornaments. They are bare-headed, with the urna, usnisa and long-lobed ears.

In addition to these, there are the Buddhas, including Dipankara, the Buddha of a past world cycle, recorded as the twenty-fourth predecessor to Gautama; the Kasyapa, Buddha of the third world cycle; Gautama of the present world cycle; Maitreya, the future Buddha; and Bhaisajyagura, the Supreme. These are also shown wearing monastic garments, without ornaments, and have the urna, usnisa and long-lobed ears.

There are many forms of Sakyamuni (Gautama Buddha). One form shows him as a child, standing, others show him seated, in various mudras, while Parinirvana shows the death of Gautama. There are also other icons known as medicine Buddhas.

The Dhyanibodhisattvas are the creators of the universe. Amongst them there are two groups: one of five and one of eight. These include Manjusri, Vajrapani, Avalokitesvara and Maitreya. Avalokitesvara, the God of Mercy, is worshipped as the patron saint of the Dalai Lama. The Dalai Lama is believed to be the living incarnation of him.

Dhyanibodhisattvas are usually shown wearing Bodhisattva ornaments. Their hair is arranged in a high chignon and they have the urna.

In addition to the more common icons mentioned before, there are numerous other manifestations, showing feminine Bodhisattvas, Taras, Dhyanibuddhas, Saktis, the Dharmapala (Defenders of the Law of Buddhism), etc.

It is difficult to examine Tibetan art from the western point of view. In Tibet the creation of beautiful things which would please the deity was primarily a form of devotion. The techniques, therefore, became part of the devotion and cannot be judged apart.

For the laity to enter a temple was an aesthetic, as well as a religious, experience. The use of beauty, the richness of precious metals and stone were all utilised to glorify the faith.

Because of the connection between art and religion the stress on quality was extremely high. The artist would have to produce only his best; nothing else would do. The religion not only controlled his life during this existence but also his future incarnations. To retain the quality of incarnation and to avoid being re-born as an inferior being he could not produce an

Colour Plate
10. South Indian bronze figure of Parvati. 18th–19th century. Ht 20 cm.

51. Tibetan bronze figure of Gautama Buddha. The wooden stand is Chinese. 18th century. Ht. 20 cm.

indifferent work. It is because of this that Tibetan art cannot simply be grouped together as mass-produced 'religious art', without being considered aesthetically. A few extremely talented artists were able to produce artistic works of the highest aesthetic order within the confines of the canonical laws.

52. Bronze figure of Avalokitesvara. The figure was originally jewelled. Not on original base. Tibet. 18th–19th century. Ht. 60 cm.

However, as the skill of individuals varied, no matter how good the intention, so did the quality of the bronzes. The infinite variety of icons, plus the complex religious and mythological backgrounds of the images, make them very attractive to collect. As investments, they are extremely good, as further examples of Tibetan art are unlikely to come out of the country since the Chinese invasion.

During the invasion and the immediate aftermath a large number of very fine objects left the country, and the writer had the pleasure of examining many of these, as they were brought out of Tibet in caravans of refugees. Many of these refugees camped in India at places along the Indo-Tibetan border, and towns such as Kalimpong, Darjeeling and Gantock became refugee centres. Some of the best objects were in the possession of monks, who brought with them icons and Thang-kas from their monasteries. Many of these works of art have now found their way into collections and museums in different parts of the world.

Apart from the numerous icons which one can collect, Tibet produced a wide range of ritual objects associated with the images. Tibetan Buddhism is probably one of the most mechanised religions that the world has ever seen. Prayers are sent to heaven in their thousands by the simplest, but most ingenious, devices. All over Tibet and the border states it is possible to see poles with long white flags. These are prayer, or luck, flags, and on to them are printed, by wooden blocks, numerous prayers. The flags flap in the wind, exposed to all conditions, and as they weather and the writing slowly disappears, so the prayers are sent on their way to heaven.

Another simple device is the prayer wheel. This can be one of four kinds: hand-operated, consisting of a small cylinder, to which is attached a chain, with a weight, which is swung on a wooden or bone handle; table-operated, consisting of a revolving cylinder within a cylinder, which can be revolved by twisting a knob at the top; temple wheels, which are large cylinders placed outside temples, usually in rows, which can be rotated when the devotee enters the temple; and a fourth variety, which has vanes attached to the cylinder, and is powered by the wind, which blows everywhere across the plains of Tibet.

Each wheel contains hundreds of prayers, sealed within it, and for each revolution it spins, that many prayers are sent spiralling on their way to the gods. The wheels are usually spun in a clockwise direction to the accompaniment of the prayer Ohm-Mani-Padme-Um—'Praise to the Jewel in the Lotus'— sometimes given obscure, abstract and philosophic interpretations.

The rosary (mala) is also used and this can be made from seed, turquoise, coral, bone (especially of holy Lamas) and snake vertebrae. For the rich, there are monks who will say their prayers for them—for a fee!

Other ritual objects of interest are the ghanta (or bell), the vajra (thunderbolt) and the purbu (ritual knife), all ritual weapons against evil.

Human bones were often used in Tibetan ritual. In a country where it was often too cold to bury the dead, the body was frequently disposed of by special persons, who took it to a high spot, where it was chopped to pieces and the flesh given to vultures. This was usually done by three people: one to chop the body, another to say prayers, and the third to make beer, to keep them from being depressed. Bones of high Lamas were sometimes left by them to their monasteries, for them to be made into ornaments, etc., for use in special rites. The skull was often made into a cup (kapala), for use in libations; or into a skull drum (damaru), used to beat pauses between services.

53. Group of Tibetan ritual objects. From left to right: table prayer wheel, hand prayer wheel, wooden printing block for preparing prayer flags, ghanta—bell.

54. Tibetan ritual objects—left, vajra or thunderbolt, (Dorsje)—right, phurbu or ceremonial dagger. Ht. 11 cm. Ht. 16 cm.

Special aprons (san mudras), the most important of the six Tantric ornamentations, were made of human bones and used in Necromantic rites by priests of the Black Hat Sect. These aprons, which are similar to those which adorn icons of dakinis, are supposed to have originated from a dakini who gave one to the great Sidhu Krsnacari during a mystic revelation.

Human thigh bones were also used in the same rites, as horns, but horns were also made of copper, sometimes long and telescopic, and at other times short, in various styles. A common type was a small, short horn, decorated with dragons, which gave sharp notes.

Mantra boxes or gau (amulet boxes) were made in embossed copper, silver and even gold, and occasionally studded with coral turquoise and semi-precious stones. Made in various sizes, they were either box-shaped, with a flat or curved roof-like top, and a container, in which a miniature icon was lodged; or an enclosed box, ornamented with scrolls and religious symbols, and inscribed on the front—some with the mystic monogram of dasakaro vasi—'The All-Powerful Ten'—a symbol of the Kalachakra Tantra (the Black Wheel). These boxes, sometimes known as god boxes, were consecrated by an incarnate Lama and worn by Tibetans to propitiate evil spirits.

Extremely fine objects were used in religious ceremonies, both within monasteries and in the ritual at the family altar. These, including the gau, were made by smiths, who could work copper as easily as gold and silver, and who were also associated with making some varieties of icons in repoussé.

The Mandala, a vessel constructed of four ornamental tiers or wheels, rising in decreasing sizes and crowned usually by a dhamacakra, or 'Wheel of Law', was used in ceremonies of Spiritual Liberation. It was usually decorated with ornate designs, with Astamangala (Eight Auspicious Symbols) and other religious symbolism. Ceremonies associated with the vessel include a vow to strive for the spiritual liberation of the Universe—'Om Vajra bhunti a hum'.

Another vessel, also decorated with auspicious emblems, was made in three tiers, which were filled with guggulu, white mustard (sarsapa) and barley, and was used in various kinds of ritual, sometimes as an offering to the god Vinayaka—Remover of Obstacles. The offerings are symbolical and represent the various manifestations of the Buddha's stages of spiritual attainment.

A simpler vessel, the Thor-nas, an ornamented bowl and cover, was used for containing sanctified rice, sprinkled while pronouncing benedictions.

Stupas, miniature shrines, shaped similar to the architectural form, were made to contain relics.

Objects used for both ecclesiastical and secular purposes include various kinds of bowls and liquid containers. An ingenious vessel, especially developed for the nomadic life of the Tibetans, was the nagbum, or inkwell, which was fitted with a special stopper, making it spillproof on travels.

Numerous kinds of teapots were made which show strong influence from Central Asia, and even Persia. Barley containers,

55. Fine repoussé copper pendant of Mahisasura–Mardini. Nepal. 19th century. 8 cm square.

butter churns, tea and beer makers and many other objects, some of high artistic merit, were made, but are outside the scope of this book. Reference to the bibliography at the back will be a help here.

Many of the religious and secular objects, although conforming to the common shape of the individual varieties of vessels and objects, provided a much-needed artistic outlet, in which the artist could express ideas which he found impossible in other spheres.

Before leaving the subject of the religious art of Tibet, some mention should be made of the votive tablets. Usually made in terracotta, they show a tradition in a material evidence of

56. Tibetan chalice or pedestal bowl. Embossed brass. 19th century. Ht. 24 cm.

which, apart from these tablets, has disappeared. They show the high skill and dexterity of the artists, though they were not intended to be seen, as they were included with the prayers and charms and sealed in images at consecration—another proof of the deep religious attitude of the Tibetan artist. The tablets portray a variety of deities and were sometimes inscribed with prayers and date of dedication. They were also made in pâpier

57. Late Tibetan tea-pot, probably from the Ladakh area. 19th century. Ht. 41 cm.

maché.

The arts of the border states were often poor copies of the main centres of Tibet and Nepal, some of the best images coming from the School of Iconology. Sikkim and other border states received many of their icons from these centres, though local craftsmen also produced both icons and utilitarian objects. However, little is known about these.

Bhutan was visited by Captain Pemberton in 1838 and in his report he does not say anything about their artistic pursuits, except for mentioning that at a place called Tassgong, large copper cauldrons were made from metal said to be obtained in the hills at the foot of Tassangsee—celebrated throughout Bhutan for superiority of manufacture.

Bronzes of all kinds are well worth collecting and make a most absorbing hobby. Although they fetch anything from $15 to $500 and upwards in the London and New York auctions, they are by no means out of the reach of the small collector. Many beautiful, and even rare, figures can be had from local auctions and antique shops for just a few dollars, or even fifty cents, but beware, do not pay high prices for any bronze until you

58. Tibetan copper tea-pot with applied embossed silver decoration. Tibet. 19th century. Ht. 55 cm.

have some idea of what you are buying. A little time spent in looking at collections in museums, handling figures in antique shops and generally taking the opportunity to see and handle as many as possible will prove most rewarding and will enable you to guard against paying too high a price for a piece. Although interest is growing in this attractive subject there are few people who know much about it. Even those who make it their business to deal in bronzes know little—although there are some notable exceptions. It is therefore advisable to be your own judge and valuer and not to rely upon others, unless he or she is an expert.

One of the commonest pitfalls in collecting bronzes is that one can often be misled by the seemingly ancient appearance of the image. This should not be taken as a criterion of age, for a bronze of the 14th century A.D. may be in mint condition, while one of the 19th century may look as if it had been made hundreds of years ago. This is due to the following reasons: Some figures were made for personal use and were constantly handled and smeared in worship with vermilion, thus wearing down the features; others were installed in altars and temples,

59. Votive tablets—left, papier mâché—right, clay. They were originally painted, the one on the right is gilt and is inscribed on the reverse. They were originally sealed within larger images, together with prayer rolls and charms. Tibet. 17th–18th century. Ht. 7·5 cm.

thereby preserving them, and those still in situ are as mint as the day they were made. Bronzes were sometimes lost or abandoned and may have been buried in the ground. These, when excavated, usually have beautiful patinas of blue or green. Forgeries are, unfortunately, most common and one must always be on the look-out for them. The bazaars and antique shops of India are full of them and many a tourist in India succombs to these attractive but worthless pieces, often going to great lengths to 'smuggle' them out of India, only to find on his return that they are fakes. Many of these figures can be found in British and American antique shops and there is still a danger of the unsuspecting collector making the same mistake.

Though these images have been given an extremely old appearance, sometimes with patina, the surface of the figures has often been treated to give them the appearance of age by immersing them in salt water, chemicals or even, sometimes, by burying them in a river bed. Occasionally acids are added to corners and other protruding parts of the image

92

to give it an appearance of great age. Green paint is sometimes used, mixed with sand and earths, to simulate the appearance of age. Most of these practices, however, can be detected by a close examination of the figure. A small scrape will often expose the new yellow brass beneath. These figures are often made by craftsmen who have no idea what will happen to the images and only carry out the instructions of their disreputable patrons. If the beginner takes precautions in examining a potential purchase, and handles as many genuine bronzes as possible, he will soon be able to distinguish between the genuine and the fake. Copies of bronzes of early schools tend to be very stiff, and often the forger may slip up by introducing features only found on sculptures of a later date. Thus, it pays to be thoroughly familiar with the different styles and costumes of the various periods. Recent bronzes tend to be rather sharp, and the edges rough, often with file marks showing on the surface. Older bronzes have usually mellowed with age, have smooth edges and are pleasant to handle.

INDIAN SCULPTURE

The most important specimens of Indian bronze art were usually meant to be placed in temples, while the stone sculptures, although often seen in museums as separate entities, were made as an integral part of the architecture of the temple. The techniques and the forms, therefore, are closely connected with architecture and masonry.

Although the collector is unlikely to have the opportunity of acquiring examples of the earlier schools of Indian sculpture, it is necessary to recount some of the earlier styles and techniques, in order to place the later schools in historical perspective.

The earliest sculpture in India comes from the Valley of the Indus, where an advanced civilisation flourished between 2500 and 1700 B.C. Although the bulk of objects excavated from the Indus Valley are of a utilitarian nature there are a few exceptionally interesting sculptures which should be described.

Probably the most famous of the Indus sculptures are the busts and heads of priest-kings or deities. These are extremely interesting because of their similarity to the sculptures of Mesopotamia and eastern Syria, although, unlike the latter, the Indus sculptures have beards, which are shown as long, straight grooves. The eyes, too, contrast strongly with the owl-like stare of the Mesopotamian types, being depicted as long, thin almonds, the general appearance being one of nobility and superiority. The Indus sculptures have a fillet around the head, and a low receding forehead, with the hair gathered at the back in a bun. They are usually shown wearing a robe with trefoil designs, draped over the left shoulder.

Apart from these heads there are two stone torsoes, excavated from Harappa, which are masterpieces of miniature sculpture. Made in grey and red stones, they both had the head and arms made separately to be fitted into sockets. These torsoes are interesting, as they resemble more the classical sculpture of later periods and may not, in fact, be contemporary with the other examples from the Indus Valley. A few minor bronze figures were made, including the figure of a dancing girl, described in a previous chapter. Numerous terracotta figurines were made in the shape of animals, toy carts and mother goddesses. The latter were shown highly stylised, heavily laden with jewellery and grotesquely overdressed. Many of the terracottas showed the strong sense of humour of the Indus artists.

The sculpture of the Indus differs from the later classical periods of Indian sculpture in that it was carved in the round, whereas all the later sculptures are essentially reliefs. The Indian sculptor never used claws, bull-noses or gouges; his only tools were flat chisels and points.

Although some examples give the appearance of being carved in the round they were still related to a ground, although they appear to stand quite free of that ground. This is basically due to two reasons: firstly, because they were an integral part of the sculptural decoration of temples, and, secondly, because of the Indian sculptor's emphasis on the convexity of the figure. Indian sculpture, therefore, contrasts strongly with the sculptures of the Classical and Hellenic Greek schools, where emphasis was placed on carving the intricate details of the muscles, tendons and various sections of the anatomy. The Indian sculptor deemed it unnecessary to use such an elaborate system and found it sufficient to divide the body into sections which were complete in themselves. This was tied up in canonical literature and poetical understanding. Indian sculpture, in many cases, is merely the expression in stone of poetical forms.

The Indian sculptor adopted a method of strip cutting, which involved cutting the stone in a series of facets, running in a continous band from the top to the bottom of the figure, producing one outline of a silhouette. The various sections of the sculpture were made to join on to each other, with only subtle linear junctions between the two masses. Each shape was an entity in itself. The whole appearance of Indian sculpture is one of supreme simplicity of form. The lesser details were never allowed to overpower the major shape. Ornaments were often reduced to patterns that were incised or raised on the major areas without altering their form. However, there are variations on this, especially in the Romano-Hellenic art of Gandhara. Clothing, too, is shown as a mere appendage to the sculpture and does not in any way interfere with the basic form. This is never more clearly shown than in the sculpture of the Gupta period, where the figures appear to be almost nude, with the clothes clinging to the body, empasising the primary form.

As mentioned earlier, Indian sculpture is built up by a series of convexities. As a rule, there are no concave forms; the hollows are merely suggested at the meeting point between two convexities. Concavities only occur on special demonic or skeletal manifestations, especially on the Disease Goddess, as the eye sockets and belly. Elsewhere they are sometimes found on free-hanging parts of draperies.

Much of Indian sculpture was intended to be finished with layers of lime plaster, in which many of the finer details were modelled, and then painted. This should be borne in mind when examining many of the granite and volcanic rock sculptures of South India and, in particular, some of the cave sculptures of Western India. In some cases where the old plaster has been preserved it gives a good idea of their original appearance.

The practice of covering and painting sculpture was also carried on in many other centres of the ancient world. Much of the Greek sculpture would appear vulgar to the modern eye in their original colours, as would the European medieval alabaster and wood carvings, which were originally in violent colours but which have now mellowed with age. In many cases, however, the addition of gesso and paint to Indian sculpture enhanced the final appearance. Unfortunately, 'freshening-up operations' often replaced the old plaster with modern plaster and painting, and this, when carried on over a number of years, ruined the appearance of the original sculptural work—and the piece would have been much better off without it. The tragedy is that this still happens today, though the various state archaeological departments and the Archaeological Survey of India do their utmost to prevent it. There was a case a few years ago when a fine 17th century terracotta temple was whitewashed!

Space was cleverly handled by the Indian sculptor, who used it as part of his composition, in the same way as he used the solid form. Some of the greatest works depend for their effect on the ingenious combination of solid form and space. The negative spaces themselves are often incorporated into sequences of simple forms.

As mentioned earlier, Indian sculpture is essentially a relief, but the artist made clever use of space and deep carving, often producing a sculpture which gave the impression of a completely free-standing figure, in no way connected with its ground. The sides of the figures were carefully exaggerated and in proportion were much greater than in life. These techniques give a tremendous effect of force, but only when viewed from the maxim position—a position calculated by the sculptor, depending upon the position the figure was to take in or on the temple. This was, perhaps, the secret of Indian sculptures, and had they to be seen from several viewpoints they would have lost much of their originality and force of movement, which would have been sacrified to detail.

Apart from appealing to the sense of vision, Indian sculpture appeals to another sense, one almost lost in the West, that of touch. The beautiful soft forms of continuous contours, carved and smoothed into stone, invite one to touch, to feel the very presence of the deity—the life force so vividly expressed in stone. This communion with the work brought about a personal identification of the viewer with the sculpture.

The rubbed-down, velvet smoothness and gradual curvature of some sculpture was also done for another reason. The strong sunlight of India falls harshly on everything and produces effects that the European artist could not imagine. Any pit-marks or angles would be strongly exaggerated by the dark, almost black, shadow cast by the Indian sun. To eliminate this, therefore, it was essential that the sculpture should have a smooth, continuous surface, either placed there during carving, or added with plaster.

Probably the use of linear form is the most attractive element in Indian sculpture. It could, perhaps, be best described as 'drawing in stone', for many of the sculptural forms are merely the translation of the linear form of painting into stone.

The combination of the forms in an entity with one continuous line of contour is essentially an Indian technique. Carved loops were cleverly used to encase the masses, giving the

Colour Plate
11. A Nepalese gilt bronze figure of a tantric deity. Part of a very large composite image. 18th–19th century. Ht. 15 cm.

impression of great space.

Indian sculpture consists of a symphony of form, the descriptions and dimensions of which were dictated by Sanskrit canonical texts. Here the connection between the poetical thought and the practical expression is strongly emphasised. The abstract idea, in fact, becomes a practical possibility. All forms must be described and, unlike Western descriptions of sculpture, which may divide the figure into forms defined in geometrical terms, the canonical texts of the Pratimamanalakshanam and the Vishnudharmottaram dictated in poetical terms what form the figure should take. The descriptions are made in metaphorical style and compare with ideals of beauty, form and texture from nature and elsewhere. For instance, the shoulder and arm should 'be like the trunk of an elephant'; the eyes of an Apsara, 'like silver fishes', and an expression of apprehension as 'fish in a dark pool'—and so on. With actual forms, they are suggested to be similar to positive forms of things. For example, the eyebrows should have the strong double curves of a bow.

As has been shown, the expressions can also be described in similar metaphorical terms, and it is therefore possible to transmit emotional force. Indian art, in fact, is similar, in many ways, to the rigidity of Indian music. Both have constant situations but the variety of expression of those situations is endless. The canonical texts not only dictated the appearance of the image but also laid down the individual measurements and proportions relative to each other, taking into account the architectural unit with which the sculpture would eventually merge.

The Indus Valley sculpture, described earlier, however interesting, must be completely separated from the later schools of Indian sculpture. The earliest pieces that concern us in an academic way are the sculptures of the Mauryan empire. Many of the sculptures of Chandragupta, fragments of which have been found at Pataliputra (near present-day Patna in Bihar) show a very strong Persian influence and may well have been the work of immigrant Persian sculptors who came to India after the fall of the Achaemenid empire.

The remains of a large hall, which contained over eighty pillars, were excavated in 1912. They show a very strong Persian influence and, although fragmentary, these pillars have a very high lustrous polish, and the general appearance of the hall is of a Persian Diwan or Apadana—audience hall.

Later, during the reign of Asoka (grandson of Chandragupta)

Colour Plate
12. Bronze image of Vishnu in three parts. South India. 18th–19th century. 97
Ht. 18 cm.

60. Fine archway from a temple incorporated in the tomb of 'Hindu Stuart', early orientalist, who is buried at South Park Street cemetery, Calcutta. The archway dates to the 10th–11th century A.D.

the Persian influence had added to it Indian thought, and was used to express typically Indian ideas. The large stone capitals erected by Asoka are of Persepolitan type but, unlike the Persian pillars, were not used to support a building but were derived from the ancient Indian custom of erecting special posts of timber or other material at various places to commemorate a great victory, to honour a deity or to mark a special sacrifice.

You must also remember the Indian mystic conception of World Axis: a pillar which separated heaven from earth.

The symbolism of Asoka's pillars was entirely Buddhist. They show extremely fine workmanship, combined with a strength and volume still reminiscent of Persian, not Indian, work.

All the Mauryan sculpture, like the Persian, was given a high lustrous polish. Some authorities, however, are of the opinion that they show more an influence of the Hellenistic school than the Persian and prefer to describe them as Perso-Hellenic. The great archaeologist, Sir John Marshall, was of the opinion that they were the work of the Bactrian artists. It is possible, of course, that Asoka may have imported Hellenistic craftsmen from Bactria, who, under the influence of Persian art, produced the peculiar style we know as Mauryan, but it is equally possible that they are the work of Indian sculptors under Perso-Hellenic influence.

The most famous of these pillars is the capital now used by the Government of India as the badge of the Republic. This consists of the fore-parts of a maned lion, facing the corners of the world. This is mounted on a drum which has, in relief, animals, separated by the cakra or wheel. The whole is supported on an inverted lotus.

Later, during the Sunga period, at a place called Bharhut, a village in Central India, a new style made its appearance. The sculpture of Bharhut in the famous red sandstone of Central India shows a new era of indigenous artistic tradition. In 1873 General Cunningham discovered the ruins of a Buddhist stupa at Bharhut, similar in plan to the Great Stupa at Sanchi. Many of the bas reliefs show scenes from the Jatakas—representations of the previous lives of Gautama Buddha.

Apart from the representations of the human-headed bull, the winged lion, the blue lotus and honeysuckle, showing influence from Persia and Western Asia, all the sculpture is purely indigenous in spirit and provides an introduction to the classical schools which were to develop over the succeeding centuries. It is not certain whether the Persian influence shown on the Bharhut stupa entered India during the Mauryan period but an examination of the sculptures points to the possibility that the motifs entered India during the pre-Asokan period. There is a pre-Mauryan or Mauryan sculpture in the Indian Museum, Calcutta, depicting a 'Bactrian' camel, honeysuckle, winged lions, geese and mother goddess, which shows that the Indian artists were capable of borrowing direct a motif of pure Bactrian origin.

The art of Bharhut is supposed to have developed from the artistic tradition started at Sanchi, and which can be seen on stupa No. 2. The sculptures here are carved in very low relief, giving the impression of drawing, without any dimensional approach. The execution of human figures is primitive. They contrast strongly with the soft-flowing curves of the floral and botanical compositions which dominate the style and have been called 'plant style' by an eminent Indian art historian. The botanical designs are also found at Bharhut, where they meander along, binding together the reliefs.

At this time the Buddha himself was never depicted in his historical life, i.e., in the incarnation of the Buddha, unlike his previous lives, shown in the Jatakas, where, when incarnate as a human form, he was shown as such.

The presence of the Buddha at Bharhut and on other sculptures of the period was only indicated by symbols, such as the Bodhi Tree, the footprints, the wheel, parasol and stupa, etc. Inscriptions confirm that the symbols stand for Gautama. Many of the reliefs of Bharhut are accompanied by descriptions, giving the title of the scene depicted. The figures of Bharhut are carved with greater depth than those from stupa No. 2 at Sanchi, though the composition was essentially one designed for a flat surface. The large single figures seem to be divorced from the main composition of the sculptures. Although a necessary part of the stories depicted, they appear expressionless and apart from the reliefs.

An interesting aspect of the sculptures is a feature often found on Egyptian reliefs: The feet (and hands, when in a position of adoration) are always portrayed sideways, showing the greatest width, with no attention being paid to anatomical accuracy, i.e., if the figure is facing front, the feet will point to the sides, thereby avoiding the complications of fore-shortening.

The sculpture at Bodhgaya in Bihar, carved about the first half of the 1st century B.C., is in the Bharhut style, but generally more advanced and more aesthetic than that of Bharhut. The contours are subtler and much softer, and the three-dimension effect more advanced than at Bharhut. This gives the figures a greater sense of movement and rhythm than the earlier examples.

Probably the greatest early Indian art was found at Sanchi on the Great Stupa. The technique, again, is similar to Bharhut, though sculptures appear only on gateways, the rails of the stupa being left plain. One of these gateways had an inscription which dated it to the second half of the 1st century B.C. Like the Bodhgaya reliefs, they are an advance upon the Bharhut style.

Already at this early date the basis of the classical school had been laid down. Carvings on the gateways of the stupa portray

61. Sandstone sculpture of a yakshi, from Sanchi, Central India. 1st century A.D. Ht. 62·5 cm.

contemporary life in India from simple jungle life to the rich and aristocratic splendour of the court. The figures are extremely natural and have a great sense of movement.

Other sculptures, also dating from the second half of the 1st century B.C., have been found at Udayagiri and Khanda-gari, near Bhuvanesvara in Orissa. Here a number of caves have their facades carved with sculptural friezes and panels. These

101

are in the Jain tradition. Some of the caves are later and possibly date towards the close of the 1st century B.C. or the beginning of the 1st century A.D. They show strong evidence of the Central Indian tradition, as at Bharhut, Bodhgaya and Sanchi, combined with the local tradition. In some cases they are in advance of the Bharhut, in that they have greater rhythm and are carved deeper than the Bharhut examples, though the workmanship is much poorer. Mathura has also produced some sculpture of this early period, which was inspired by the same artistic tradition of the Central Indian school.

In Western India, too, there was a great development in sculpture at this time, parallel to, but with some influence from, the Central Indian school. There, a tradition began of rock-cut caves and temples. The oldest of these caves are at Bhaja, near Poona, which have reliefs going back to the 2nd century B.C., and which recall the Bharhut tradition, but show powerful naturalism. Unlike the Bharhut examples, which are Buddhist, the sculptures portray Hindu deities, such as Surya and Indra. South India also began to produce sculptures during this period. Some of the earliest come from Jaggayyapeta, about thirty miles north-west of Amaravati. These, like the examples on stupa No. 2 at Sanchi, are extremely shallow and almost like linear sketches. However, the southern movement is characterised by the preference for the elongation of limbs and for their slim modelling. This development is shown clearly in the early sculpture of Amaravati in the 1st century B.C.

Further south there is some early sculpture from Gudimallan. This is a unique representation of the Siva-linga, showing Siva, standing on a crouched yaksha, carved on the lower section of the lingam. The figure, with its vigorous body, may be related to the Jaggayyapeta school, or possibly even to the Central Indian of this period.

The Greco-Roman Buddhist school of Gandhara will provide the earliest examples of sculpture that the collector will be able to obtain. Most of the pieces of the earlier schools were recovered by excavation and are in museums. However, the collector is extremely fortunate, in that sufficient examples of Gandharan art exist, both in, and outside, India, for him to take an active interest. Perhaps one of the most interesting of Indian schools, it reflects a strong Hellenic influence but expresses purely Indian ideas of Buddhism.

The first figures of Buddha himself were sculpted by the school as early as the 2nd century A.D. The most popular themes were representations of the Buddha, the Bodhisattvas and the Jatakas. The school, which lasted from the 1st to the 6th century A.D., greatly influenced the early sculpture of China through the trade routes of Central Asia.

Gandhara was the name applied to the region around Peshawar on the north-west frontier. Its most important cities were Purushapura (Peshawar) and Pushkalabati (Charsadda). The districts of Hazara, Rawalpindi and Taxila (ancient Takshasila) were sometimes included in the province, producing works in the Gandharan manner. The style later became stereotyped and spread over a large area, including Buluchistan, Afghanistan and even Central Asia.

Although Buddha never went to Gandhara, it was converted to Buddhism by the emperor Asoka in the 3rd century B.C.

During the 1st century A.D., Buddhist sages wrote texts connecting local sites with the Jatakas, and Gandhara became a sacred region. Herodotus recalled that the Gandharoi (Gandharans) supplied a contingent to the Persian emperor Xerxes for his invasion of Greece. Darius (*circa* 516 B.C.) mentions Gandhara as one of his subject nations in the Bisutun inscription. Part of the Achaemenian empire it was conquered in 327 B.C. by Alexander the Great. During the Mauryan period it was consolidated with the rest of the empire. It was later conquered by the Bactrian kingdom—which, at that time, although cut off from Greece, had preserved a Hellenistic culture. In the 1st century B.C. it was conquered by the Kushans, who ruled it until the White Huns overran North India in the 5th century A.D.

It was during the reign of the Kushan emperor, Kanishka, in the 2nd century A.D., that Buddhism reached its zenith. The sculptures of Gandhara express indigenous Buddhist ideas but are executed in a pseudo-Hellenistic style. This influence from the Mediterranean took many years to reach Gandhara by way of Iran, but was reinforced by Roman influence from the eastern centres of the Roman Empire, as a result of trade established between Rome, Western Asia and India in the 1st century A.D. This is why we should, perhaps, regard it more as a Romano-Buddhist school, as many of the Hellenistic ideals had been Romanised before they influenced the Indian sculptors. The widespread use of the Corinthian, rather than the Ionic, capital is paralleled in Roman architecture. The Gandharan type of Corinthian capital appears as far away as Baalbeck and Palmyra. A study of Gandharan architecture shows closer affinity to the Roman than to the Greek. Acanthus foliage also appears on some sculptures.

During the first phase of Gandharan sculpture, 2nd to 4th century A.D., direct carving in the local schist stone was favoured, while later, from the 4th to the 6th century A.D., terracotta, wood and stucco were more popular. The stone, which is of a soft, bluish-grey colour, was quarried in the hills of Swat and Buner, north of Peshawar. It was described by Asvaghosa, a contempory poet, as 'blue as an elephant's ear'. The sculpture was almost entirely Buddhist, and the monuments were covered with sculptured figures and reliefs of all sizes. Unlike those of Bharhut and Sanchi, the Gandharan sculptors made a real attempt at perspective. When a group of figures was represented, the figures in the foreground were sculpted almost in the round, while those at the back were left flat. This avoided the possibility that the more distant figures would cast shadows over those supposed to be in the foreground. This technique deteriorated as time went on, until the front and back figures were all on the same plane.

The figures of Buddha in Gandhara are shown wearing a toga-like robe which reaches below the knees. The folds are well defined and were produced by carving parallel and horizontal curves in relief. The limbs are generally thick, and even plump. The head is strongly influenced by Greek renderings of the head of Apollo. The features are full; the eyes are half-open, indicating divine peace; the nose is almost Roman, its lines continuing upwards to form stylised brows. There is an urna on the forehead; the lips are well proportioned, with strongly curved lines; the ears are pendulous. The hair is shown long and wavy and the cranial protruberance, or usnisa, disguised by an adaptation of the top-knot, similar to the krobylos of the Greek sun god. Later in South India this protruberance was shown as a lotus flower or flame. A halo is placed behind the head. The total height of the figure is in the proportion of five heads, as were the figures of the late Roman sculpture.

The iconometric form of Buddha which developed in Gandhara was later to spread to other parts of the Buddhist world, where it was to form the foundation of all future representations of the Master. Although the Gandharan sculptors were the first to produce an anthromorphic image of Buddha, it was the Gupta artist who inspired the figures with the mystic and dynamic spirit of the Enlightened One. Perhaps the earliest dateable representation of the Buddha is the figure on a casket found at Bimaran in Afghanistan, which may date to the 1st century B.C.

The Buddha or Bodhisattva statues can be full life-size, though they are generally half life-size. The size of the figures on the reliefs varies between 1 inch and 6 inches.

In addition to the figure of Buddha, generally thought to be borrowed from Greek figures of Apollo, other classical figures were borrowed, such as Heracles, Athena, etc. Heracles was transformed into Indra or Siva, Panchika or Vajrapani; Athena sometimes became a yaksha, or female harem guard—and so on. The figures of the Bodhisattvas, however, seem to be purely indigenous inventions, the loin-cloth, turban, hair style and princely ornaments being characteristic of the costume of princes of the period. The production of images of Buddha in a leg-locked yoga posture was also an original invention.

The reliefs were mainly used to decorate the walls of the stupas and depict scenes from the life of the Buddha, the most popular scenes being the Conception, the Miraculous Birth, the Great Departure, the Great Enlightenment, and numerous other miracles. The separate figures were intended for the niches in the walls of stupas and monasteries.

As in later schools, much of the sculpture was meant to be covered in plaster, painted and sometimes even gilded. However, few examples with any traces of colour survive.

There is still discussion as to whether the figures with the more Hellenised features are the earlier. This is open to debate but from the stylistic point of view it is possible to see a change, both in facial features and in the treatment of the drapery, and on this basis one would place the figures with strong Hellenistic features as earlier, the later examples having lost their expression to almost stereotyped features. The folds of the drapery, too, become simple string-like attachments. Later, when the centres of artistic production shifted to areas where schist was not available, the sculptors expressed themselves mainly in the media of stucco and terracotta. At Taxila in Sind a large number of stucco and terracotta heads have been found, and it was probably one of the main centres of production.

Although the sculpture is later than the Mauryan and Sunga dynasties, it was in no way a continuation of the early tradition. It contributed to the later classical schools only inasmuch as it (together with the Andhran and Central Indian schools) contributed to the evolution of the Gupta style, which laid down the true Indian ideas that were to influence all later schools of art.

The collector will find a wide selection of Gandharan art,

62. Stucco head of the Buddha, Gandhara. North-west India. 4th–5th century A.D. Ht. 28·5 cm.

depending upon the amount he wishes to spend. The most common are reliefs and fragments of reliefs, figures of Buddha and Bodhisattvas, heads of Buddha and Bodhisattvas (both in stone and stucco), miniature stupas and bases of figures.

63. A Gandhara grey schist rectangular block, the base of a large figure. Each face carved with a figure of Buddha seated in the attitude of meditation flanked by an attendant on either side. 2nd–3rd century A.D. Ht. 12·5 cm.

Bases are square and have scenes carved around the sides and a hole in the centre for the figure to slot into.

Mathura, an ancient and prosperous city, situated, as it was, at the converging point of trade routes, became a centre of artistic activity, where sculptural works were produced almost uninterrupted until the medieval period. The influence of Mathura reached far and wide and sculptures in its distinctive style have been found in many places in India.

The school of Mathura is extremely important in the study of Indian sculpture. In early times it was closely linked with the Central Indian school, the remains of which, from Bharhut and Sanchi, have already been described.

The importance of Mathura begins in the 1st century A.D., contemporaneous with that of Gandhara. It is at Mathura that the cult of iconographic images of deities begins to shape a new conception of Indian art. Here, reliefs begin to give way to the principal expression of the human figure. This necessitated a change in techniques. New ideas of artistic composition were formed around the figure, according to iconographic

107

dictates. Formulas were invented for the composition of the primary figure and the addition of secondary figures in the form of attendants—the well-known image stele had been born.

Development in the modelling from these early figures can be seen by the introduction of articulation and greater contours On figures of Buddha the usnisa is shown as a spiral and the urna as a raised dot on the centre of the forehead. Bodhisattvas are found, and Jain and Brahminical sculptures were also executed. Although great experimentation seems to have taken place in the development of iconographic details, the mystic spirit and dynamic force of the deities seems totally absent and does not make itself felt until much later. It is, perhaps, possible to detect the influence of Gandhara in the treatment of the drapery on a few of the sculptures of Buddha. Mathuran sculpture, however, is completely indigenous in expression.

Apart from figures and groups, etc., Ayagapattas were made. These were votive slabs erected in Jain shrines.

Very fine nude, or semi-nude, female figures were sculpted on rail pillars. These figures of yakshinis or apsaras are shown in non-religious activities, such as toilet scenes, etc. They seem to bear some relationship to sculptures of yakshinis at Bharhut, Sanchi and Bodhgaya, though they are far in advance sculpturally.

The development of sculptural plasticity led to the creation of female figures which had strong erotic or sensual overtones. These figures are beautifully conceived and sculpted. Emphasis is placed both on the expression of movement and the position of the body, often achieved by a subtle change of angle at the hips and by the expression, sometimes exaggerated, of the physical attractions, such as the breasts, etc.

The other great artistic school of the period is to be found at Amaravati in the Deccan, which lasted for several hundred years, until the decline of the Andhran dynasty. The foundation had been laid as early as the 2nd century B.C., when the school of Vengi had made tentative experiments at Jaggayyapeta, the reliefs of which have already been mentioned. The true centre of the Andhran school was at Amaravati, although sculptural remains have been found at Nagarjunakonda. The Great Stupa itself lies a little to the south of the town, and about half a mile west lie the ruins of Dhanyakataka, the provincial capital of the Satavhanas, the ruling family of the Andhras. Amaravati once the finest monument of the Buddhist

64. Sandstone sculpture of a yakshi (tree spirit). From a Jain stupa at Mathura, Northern India. Kushan dynasty. 2nd century A.D. Ht. 51 cm.

world now lies as a sprawling ruin.

The sculpture production of Amaravati was prolific, probably producing more than any other school of Indian art. A major collection of the sculpture can be seen in the British Museum, London. Another collection is in the Government Museum in Madras. In comparison to the classical schools of Europe they rank with the Elgin marbles.

There has been much discussion as to the date of the Amaravati sculptures. Generally there are two schools of thought, one favouring 'the long chronology', the other, 'the short chronology'. The 'long chronology' prefers to date the sculpture of the earliest phase as early as the 1st, or even the 2nd, century B.C., and continues it for several hundred years, the mature style occurring in the 2nd to 3rd century A.D. The 'short chronology' places the majority of the sculpture in the relatively short period of the 2nd to the 4th century A.D.

Arguments against the 'long chronology' include the theory

that there was not sufficient wealth or social organisation to erect the monuments, and also that there was no certainty that the inhabitants were even Buddhists. The advocates of the 'short chronology' also maintain that the early sculptures cannot be based on comparisons with the stupas of Northern India and the temples of north-west Deccan—but *they* must be reconsidered in the light of the 'short chronology'. Whichever is accepted it is only of academic interest to the collector, as he is unlikely to find examples of the school on the open market. It is interesting, however, to note that the representations of the Buddha at Amaravati in the first phase are symbolic a practice which, though found at Bharhut, disappears in the art of Mathura and Gandhara.

In comparison with the early reliefs of Jaggayyapeta the Amaravati reliefs are cut slightly deeper and the figures appear to be more substantial. The costume is similar to some found on the Sanchi reliefs. The compositions are iconographically more complicated than those found at Gandhara or Mathura.

Inscriptions discovered at Amaravati record that during the second and third quarters of the 2nd century A.D. extensive alterations and additions were made to the stupa and during this period the figures are marked by an exuberance not found in the earlier sculptures. The human figure seems to attain the greatest importance, especially the male figure, and the reliefs are deeper, with greater contours. In spite of this they are delicately modelled and sensitive. The motifs of the reliefs are, of course, Buddhist and depict scenes of Buddha and Jatakas. Female figures also occur at Amaravati. With the carvings sensuous and delicate they give a strong sense of presence. The heavy hips, full bust and amorous expression contrast with the figures of Mathura in that those at Amaravati are more refined. The compositions as a whole seem to have a strong sense of movement, bound together by rhythmic lines. Group figures are sculpted on a number of planes and attempts are made to produce illusions of great depth. This is achieved in various ways. Often the main figure is removed to the background, enticing the viewer to penetrate beyond the outer figures, thus giving an illusion of depth. Sometimes foreshortening and over-secting are used to great effect. Occasionally the figures are shown at various angles, which also gives an illusion of depth.

Later, in the 3rd century A.D., sculpture gradually deteriorated into a profusion of interlacing and interwined figures in wild and frenzied movements.

The figure of the Buddha occurs at Amaravati both standing and seated, on reliefs, as well as isolated statues. The treatment of the drapery seems closely related to the Mathura images. The head is more of a narrow, oval form, but with a spiral usnisa. The hair is represented by snail-shelled curls. The lines of the drapery are flowing and orderly, emphasising the form of the figure. A peculiarity of the images of the Buddha from the Amaravati area is that there is a heavy fold at the bottom of the outer garment, where it falls above the ankles.

The Amaravati style extended to Ceylon through its commercial and religious missions. Buddhist images in the Andhra style have been found as far away as Dong-Duong, Indo-China.

It will be noticed that all the sculpture described up to now and, indeed, all the examples of later schools, were connected with architecture, and this must be borne in mind when examining and appreciating Indian sculpture as a whole. In nearly every case it was part of the decorative feature of architecture, only on exceptional occasions being produced as individual pieces. This applies equally to the standing figures sculpted almost free-standing and to the panel stele. Both were made to fit into niches and, in the case of the latter, as additions to the internal and external sculptural and architectural effect of the buildings. This effect could be achieved by the medium of terracotta, as well as stone. Terracotta temples were built during the 16th, 17th and 18th centuries, especially at Birbhum in Eastern India.

Although the school did not long survive the fall of the Andhran dynasty it had great influence on the later Hindu schools of the South.

We now come to the golden age of Indian art, the Gupta period, which takes its name from Chandragupta, crowned king of kings at Pataliputra in A.D. 320. Although Gupta sculpture seems to belong to a completely different sphere it is the logical product of the classical sculpture of Mathura and Amaravati. For the purpose of description we can take the period to extend from the 4th to the close of the 6th century A.D., although a strong Gupta influence continued to be felt until the 8th century A.D.

With the advent of this new period the sculptors seem to have mastered the plasticity of form and were then able to impart other qualities missing from the earlier works. This quality is almost a sculptural breath of life. The Gupta artists were working to much higher ideals. It was a period of inter-

111

action between literature, science and the arts, which resulted in the canonical basis for many of the later images and created new aesthetic ideals. The art became, in fact, the vehicle of both intellectual and spiritual concepts. The human figure was now all-important in sculpture, unlike the earlier representations of figures at Mathura and Amaravati. The figure became supreme; all other decorative motifs, secondary. In this way it was almost superhuman, an expression in visible form of invisible concepts. It was a modification of realistic form to express abstract ideas.

As the figure became all-important it took on all the primitive rhythm previously attributed to the many botanical motifs which surrounded the figures of the earlier schools. It was, perhaps, this rhythm which supplied the figure with its vitality.

Images of the Buddha are carved with an expression of supreme spiritual calm, which emanates from the sculpture, unlike any other figures carved before or after the Gupta period. Preference is given to the youthful form, as the canons prescribed that the gods and goddesses should always be shown in forms of perpetual youth. This was applied to all images, whether Buddhist, Brahmanical or Jain, and also affected the portrayal of ordinary men and women. All superfluous jewellery and ornamentation, popular in the earlier periods, was removed, simplicity being the rule, and great emphasis was placed on the continuation and smooth flow of the lines and contours. Anything that interfered with this was removed, including drapery, which was reduced to near-transparency, all folds clinging to and emphasising the anatomical form.

It was at this time that the sculptural rendering of poetical ideas, mentioned earlier, began to take shape and the metaphorical descriptions began to be expressed. Thus we have another example of the influence of nature, which, although absent from the reliefs, is expressed as similes to the various parts of the human body. It is now, also, that the figures should more correctly be looked upon as images in the true sense, conforming to the canons, and being carved in certain fixed poses dictated as asanas, mudras or hastas. These poses will be found described in the chart at the back of the book. These postures and gestures were formulated to symbolise various attitudes and images. For instance, the Dhyanamudra, often associated with Buddha images, is a gesture of deep meditation. The Bhumisparsa mudra with Enlightenment and the Dhar-

Colour Plate

13. Very fine Tibetan gilt bronze figure of bodhisattva avalokitesvara. The figure was originally jewelled. Ht. 19 cm.

macakra mudra signifies the turning of the wheel of law as the first sermon in the deer park at Isipatna (Sarnath).

Two great centres of Gupta sculpture were founded at Mathura and Sarnath and spread rapidly to Madhyadesa and Eastern India. It also had great influence on the contemporary art of the Deccan.

Although probably the greatest of Gupta sculptures are images of the Buddha the period also saw a revival of a new cult of Vishnu, with Krishna as the exponent and divine teacher (of the Vaishnava doctrine).

Buddhism at this time was very little different from the other sects of Hinduism and was gradually being absorbed into the Hindu ideals, which finally led to the disappearance of Buddhism from India.

During the Gupta period the form of the Buddha is entirely Indian, the different parts of the body being portrayed according to the metaphorical description contained in the lakshanas. However, the influence of Gandhara can be seen quite clearly in the technique used on some of the figures. There is a sharp definition which separates the eye sockets from the brow, similar to that seen on Gandharan Buddhas, but unlike the latter, the Mathuran examples avoid the mask-like expressions found at Gandhara by producing a swelling of the face, which gives the figures a feeling of warmth. The hair differs from the Gandharan in that it is shown as small, tight curls.

Many of the Jain images, both of the Gupta and later periods, seem to be modelled on the figures of Buddha produced at this time, an indication that there was little distinction made by the sculptors, who produced works for all the religions.

At Sarnath, the Chunar sandstone, first used during the Mauryan period, was used to make the numerous figures of Buddhas and Bodhisattvas that decorated the stupas and viharas. Most of the Sarnath Buddhas have an almost abstract appearance, produced by over-simplification of the surfaces. One of the most beautiful aspects of these images is the contrast of the simplicity of the figures with the intricate carving of the haloes.

Perhaps one of the greatest pieces of all Gupta sculpture was found in the ruins at Sarnath. It shows the Buddha seated in a yoga posture, his hands turning the wheel of law—the dharmacakra mudra. The image is interesting because although it preserves the simplicity of the figure, the background slab is carved intricately with monsters or yalis. It is the final stage in the transformation of the representations of the early stories of

Colour Plate
14. A finely modelled bronze figure of Tara, seated in the ardhaparyanka pose on the padmasana. The face and hair shows traces of gilding and paint. Tibet. 17th–18th century. Ht. 18 cm.

113

the Buddha's life, which were first shown in the reliefs of Gandhara as portrayals of the actual event. At Sarnath this pictorial element is removed to the base of the figure of Buddha, the enlarged image in the dharmacakra mudra being all-important.

As mentioned earlier, the Gupta sculptures were not limited to the artistic centres of Mathura and Sarnath, but as the influence spread across India, other centres produced sculptures in the Gupta style. One of the most monumental of these sculptures is the colossal figure of the boar, avatar, of Vishnu at Andayagiri, Bhopal.

During the last quarter of the 5th century the Gupta empire disintegrated under the fierce conquests of the Huns and allied tribes from Central Asia, who overran Northern India.

Gupta figures, although rare, can sometimes be acquired, but the collector should always examine the sculpture carefully, as many examples are, in fact, later than the true Gupta period and are only in the Gupta style. However, this does not detract from their aesthetic quality. Some authorities have overcome this difficulty by including the reign of Harsha of Kananj (A.D. 606 to 647) in the Gupta period. It will be the period immediately following the Gupta of which the collector will be able to obtain the most examples.

For the purpose of describing the later schools—post-Gupta and medieval—it will be best to divide India into regions. In this way we will be able to show the individual regional developments, as opposed to a national chronology. By the 7th century in Northern India there was a change in religion. Buddhism had virtually disappeared and only in Bengal do we find it surviving, until destroyed by the Mohammedan invasions in the 12th century.

In Eastern India the effect of the Gupta period was felt for some time. Though the art of the East seems to be more dynamic, with a greater sense of feeling and sublety, it does not disappear during the later periods, which failed to equal the creations of Sarnath. The period between the end of the Gupta and beginning of the Pala period is marked by an array of miscellaneous sculpture from different places. A group of stone sculptures from Paharpur in north Bengal was probably made in the 7th century. These sculptures, in the basement wall of the great temple, retain much of the earlier Gupta feeling. They are sensitively modelled but do not match the technique of Sarnath. The chronological continuity of the groups of Paharpur sculptures shows the gradual change from the classical ideals of the Gupta to the more emotional and dynamic qualities of the Eastern school. Often the compositions are extremely powerful but the technique is rather crude, belonging more to a folk medium than to classical artistic schools. Terracotta sculpture is also found at Paharpur, although later than the sculptures previously mentioned, and seems more at home in expressing the vigorous ideals. These sculptures, in fact, provide the introduction to the classical school of the Palas, who came into power in Eastern India in the 8th century.

Pre-Pala and early Pala sculptures are rare and the collector is unlikely to come across examples, as the majority of sculptures from Eastern India will fall between the 9th and 12th centuries A.D. In Eastern India the gradual change from the classical to the medieval school is clearer to see than in any other part of India.

The Pala and Sena dynasties (A.D. 730 to 1197) succeeded the empire of Harsha in the Gangetic Valley. The Palas, who were great patrons of the arts, were adherents of Tantric Buddhism, which differed from Mahayana Buddhism, and which included many traits of Hinduism. It was the basis of the Buddhism that was imported into Tibet by Padmasambhava, but under the Palas it gradually assimilated aspects of Saivism and Vaishnavism (the worship of Siva and Vishnu respectively), until it finally disappeared in the 12th century. The last great centre of Buddhism was at Nalanda in Bihar—not only a university city but also a great artistic centre.

As in earlier periods, the sculpture is associated with architecture and adorned temples, stupas, etc. Sculptures were made at various centres in Eastern India, including Bihar, Orissa and Bengal, although Bihar and Bengal must be treated as a separate artistic centre from that of Orissa. One of the centres of production, Dinajpur, is now in East Pakistan, and the Dacca Museum has a fine array of Pala images in stone, metal and wood. The black basalt, used in these sculptures, which was quarried from Rajmahal, is interesting, in that it is soft when first quarried but hardens soon after. The basalt was found at many sites in Bengal, including Nalanda. The technique is usually deep, although little attempt is made to produce under-cuts. Definition is sharp and great attention is paid to ornaments, especially on the later examples.

The common Pala sculpture is a stele and ranges in height from approximately ten inches to several feet. Unfortunately, many of the later Pala sculptures are stereotyped and show little individual inspiration. Often attempts are made to express, in stone, the rococo style found on some of the bronzes.

The figures of a Pala sculpture can best be described as images in the true sense of the word. They are entirely dictated

65. Pala stone sculpture depicting the marriage of Siva and Parvati. 10th century A.D. Ht. 62·5 cm.

66. Pala stone stele of Vishnu, flanked by his consorts Lakshmi and Saraswati. 11th–12th century A.D. Dinajapur. Ht. 55 cm.

by canonical texts. The stele, the common form of sculpture, is usually a flat slab, with the top curving like a pointed arch. The main figure is shown much larger than the secondary figures, although they, too, may be gods or goddesses. For example, statues of the god Vishnu commonly show him standing, with four arms, holding his usual attributes, with the small attendant figures of Lakshmi and Saraswati. The figures are usually shown on a double lotus base. Vishnu, or the main figure, on some steles, is sometimes shown with the torso and legs cut away from the back of the stele, giving an illusion of depth and of a free-standing figure. The back of the steles is frequently carved with a demon's mask, apsaras and foliage. Sometimes the figures of devotees are carved beside the attendant figures and, towards the base of the sculpture, figures of the donor.

Common images include Buddha, Vishnu, Saraswati, Siva, Durga, Manasa (the Snake Goddess) and Surya (the Sun God). Pala sculpture is very distinctive and can rarely be confused with other schools of Indian art.

Drapery on the early figures, especially Buddha, is strongly

67. Black stone sculpture of the goddess Saraswati. Pala, Eastern India. 11th–12th century A.D. Ht. 58 cm.

68. Pala black stone sculpture depicting the god Vishnu flanked on either side by his consorts Lakshmi and Saraswati. 11th century A.D. Bengal. Ht. 60 cm.

nude, but this is an illusion, the actual drapery clinging to the body, emphasising the anatomical form. However, comparison between the Gupta and the Pala techniques will show the distinction between the two schools. The earlier examples of Pala images are not sculpted as deeply as the later ones and look like true reliefs, rather than semi-free-standing figures.

Apart from the stele, the collector will find architectural fragments, carved with reliefs. The figures are usually cleverly composed to fit the available space.

Buddhism was shattered by the impact of the Moslem invasion at the close of the 12th century. Thousands of Buddhist monks were slaughtered. The few that escaped were scattered throughout India. This invasion not only destroyed Buddhism but also, to a certain extent, art, both Hindu and Buddhist, over a large area of Northern India. In Orissa, however, which was not completely conquered until the 16th century, the tradition continued for a time, some of the best work being produced in the 13th century. A degenerate form of this tradition continues to the present day, but has been diverted from monumental sculpture to finicky carvings in sandstone. In Bihar and Bengal, during the later periods, there was a mild revival in the Hindu tradition. Sculptural works in stone and terracotta were produced in increasing numbers from the 17th century onwards. Some very fine terracotta temples exist in India, with notable examples in Bengal.

Unlike other regions in India many of the temples in Bengal were built of brick. These buildings differed architecturally from the stone examples, due to the choice of terracotta as a medium. Sculpturally, too, they developed their own peculiar style. The temples were covered with bricks and tiles, and the artist found it difficult to express the same boldness of relief found on the stone temples. The decorative terracottas that adorn these temples are extremely interesting and there are some wonderful examples that the collector can obtain. The motifs are drawn from Hindu sources, such as the Ramayana, the loves and lives of Krishna, etc., but also include the revival of the use of flora and fauna in decorative designs, where Moslem influence can sometimes be seen.

Some of the best examples of terracotta bricks come from Jessore, Khulna and Birbhum. The figures are modelled in low relief, in clever compositions which fit them into the shape of the brick. Some of the large figures are made in more than one section. The modelling is full of vitality and has a great sense of movement and plastic form. Dancing figures, celestial

69. Pala black stone stele of Manasa, the snake goddess. 10th–11th century A.D. Ht. 50 cm.

70. Late stone sculpture of Ganesha. 17th–18th century A.D. Eastern India. Ht. 17 cm.

musicians and deities are popular. They are often modelled within an arched niche and framed by decorative borders. In many cases the execution of the figure is in a similar style to the bronzes of the period.

The revival of flora and fauna motifs echoes some of the great traditions of earlier times, though the foreign elements of Mohammedanism have often left their mark. Popular motifs include birds, especially geese, creepers, deer and monkeys, and many examples are confined entirely to designs from nature.

The composition of the terracotta bricks has a vitality and rhythm which, from the point of view of pure design, is often superior to the stone reliefs.

Wood was also widely used, both for the erection of domestic and religious structures, as well as sculptural reliefs, and even for making images. These sculptures were often finished by colouring.

Wooden sculpture was produced from an early date and some fine examples of the 13th century have been recovered from Vikrampur, near Dacca. However, the collector will

71. Terracotta temple brick. Eastern India. 17th–18th century A.D. Ht. 18 cm.

find that the majority of wood sculpture that he will come across will fall into the 17th, 18th and 19th centuries. Many fine reliefs are, in fact, found on architectural fragments. The carving is often very shallow and sometimes open-work (fretwork). These two techniques can also be found together on a single piece.

The earliest architecture and sculpture of the Indo-Aryan style, which succeeded the Gupta, can be found at Bhuvanesvar in Orissa. The style, which lasted from the 8th to the 13th century, under the Chalukya dynasty, is graceful and simple, and the carving of the features extremely fine. Faces often have a subtle smile. The noses of the female figures are much longer than those of other styles. The oldest sculpture comes from Bhuvanesvar and is in sandstone, while the later

72. Interesting terracotta temple brick. The pose of the figure has been carefully thought out to fit within the border. Twenty-four parganas. Bengal. 18th century. Ht. 17·5 cm.

pieces seem to be in chlorite. Many of the Bhuvanesvar carvings (500—600) show erotic scenes from the Treatise of the Kamasutra. The work on some of the minor ancillary figures is extremely pleasing, the sculptors having greater freedom in expressing themselves with these than with the canonical images of the deities. Probably the greatest sculptures of the Orissan school occur at the Temple of the Sun at Konarak. This unfinished building is in the form of a gigantic solar car or chariot, drawn by horses. Due to the proximity of the sea and the fact that they were carved in a ferruginous sandstone the Konarak sculptures are usually found very eroded. Many of the figures are of an erotic nature and again illustrate themes from the Kamasutra. Generally the sculptures show a mastery of curves and composition, the female figures sur-

73. Terracotta temple brick. Birbhum, Eastern India. 18th century. Ht. 16 cm.

passing all others.

The Orissan sculptures are a natural progression from the first great sculptural tradition of the Gupta period. The Indo-Aryan school was also established at an early date in Central India, and probably the greatest examples come from the temples at Khajuraho, dedicated to the Chandella Rajput kings. Only twenty of these temples survive out of the original eighty-five. Dedicated to Siva, Vishnu and Jainism, the sculptures again show erotic themes, symbolising the union with the divine. The temples are literally covered with the finest of sculptures. Figures of the female form were very popular and reached unsurpassed heights. Many of the figures stand on their own platform and are carved almost completely in the round. The play upon curves and contours injects the figures with great vitality and warmth. The body is carved with considerable skill, emphasising the fullness and roundness of the flesh, the breasts and belly contrasting with the exaggerated lines of the arms and legs.

74. Stone sculpture of Ambika. Orissa. 12th–13th century A.D. Ht. 40 cm.

Although similar to the Orissan sculptures, those of Khajuraho constitute a new and original style. Apart from the female
figures, much use was made of fantastic animals, nagas, couples
and celestial musicians. It is a great shame that the majority
of the sculptures from Orissa and Khajuraho are of an erotic
nature and, for this reason, cannot be illustrated. Procreation,
to the Indian, was a most important act and of deep religious
significance. It was closely connected not only with religious,
but with profound philosophical ideas, whether ritual or
esoteric, and therefore the Indian sculptor felt no shame, but
completely justified, in illustrating many erotic themes. These
sculptures can be ranked amongst the great works of Indian
art.

The indigenous local tradition of the Gangetic plains, which
favoured heavy and sturdy forms, had been submerged during
the Gupta period, but re-emerged during post-Gupta times
to become an important ingredient in the art form. This is
shown in the tendency to sculpt the figures with heavier,
broader forms.

Fine examples of Central Indian sculpture, dating from the

8th century, can be collected. Much of the earlier work, carved in buff, grey and red sandstone, is badly eroded. Subjects include representations of Vishnu, Siva, Devi, Indra, Brahma, Yakshinis, Surasundari (celestial beauty) and Mithuna (lovers) and many others. There are some very fine compositions of dancing females. The figures show an abundance of curves. The face is oval, with a long, straight nose and high arched brows. The eyes are fish-shaped, with well-defined lids, though the lids are sometimes ignored in preference to pupils. Lips are small but thick, with the upper lips bow-shped. The limbs are fully modelled but with little or no anatomical detail. The legs are a little stiff, and both male and female figures are adorned with elaborate jewellery. Female figures are carved with full round breasts.

During the 14th century, sculpture was carved in chloretic schist and polished. The stele was a common form. The figures were stiffly carved in open-work; the features rigid, almost metallic.

A splendid example of what befell Hindu culture at the onslaught of the Moselm invasion can be seen at the Qutb Mosque, Delhi, which has in it the material ravaged from approximately thirty temples.

Gujerat, under the Solanki dynasty, grew very prosperous and numerous temples and sculptures of great delicacy were commissioned. Unfortunately, most of them suffered from the wrath of the Moslem iconoclastic raids. Mahmud of Ghazni was a fanatical anti-idolist, and in 1025 raided and smashed one of the finest of Gujerati temples, Somanatha Patan. Although later restored, it was sacked again in the 13th century. The sculptures reflect the wealth of the period. They are extremely detailed and sometimes so deep that they give the effect of pierced and applied metal-work. It is possible that this carving was often achieved by abrasion, rather than by direct cutting.

The Baroque carvings of the Jain temples at Mount Abu could perhaps be best described as the pinnacle of the Gujerat style. They were carved in white marble, which had to be brought up from the valleys. Because the sculptors paid such attention to elaborate and delicate carving and fretting, the texture of the stone is lost. The carvings seem to separate themselves from the very medium in which they were conceived. Figures are carved with great delicacy, and foliage is used to great effect.

There are many Jain images and stelae, carved in white

and black marble, which are extremely interesting and well worth collecting.

During later years, sculptures continued to be made, but in a subdued, often rigid, form. Sculptures in white marble were also produced in the 17th to the 19th century. At Mamallapuram in Gwalior there are some fine examples of sculptures in the late Indo-Aryan style. These deeply cut reliefs have been badly damaged by invaders, but what remains echoes strongly early Gupta workmanship.

During the 7th and 8th centuries there was an explosion of artistic works in the Deccan.

Sculptures of the period are difficult to obtain as they mostly form part of the rock-cut temples which were fashionable at the time. The artists took full advantage of these settings to produce vibrant and dynamic compositions.

The main centres during the early phase were at Udayagiri and Badami, and during the later phases, at the caves of Ellora, Aurangabad and Elephanta. The sculptures, mainly expressing themes of the life of Siva, are on a massive scale.

In the Ellora caves the deities seem to have been endowed with the actual force of life and are almost animated. A dramatic effect is created by recessing the reliefs deep into the walls. When the light falls upon them they seem to emerge from the depths.

Although the Aurangabad caves are Buddhist they also exploit the same ideas that are found at Ellora.

Contemporary with the fabulous rock-cut temples are the free-standing temples of Alampur, Pattadakal Ahole and Mahakata. These temples, experiments in structural form, were richly endowed with sculptural works, embellishing the architectural form. The sculptural works of Pattadakal and Alampur are interesting, in that they blend the rock-cut techniques to a new conception of the slim physique—an echo of earlier times. The result is a dynamic, powerful figure, with a slender body and ease of movement.

The sculptural forms of the Deccan were strongly influenced by the artistic style of the Pallavas.

It is interesting to reflect that, although these cave temples seem to inspire the viewer to marvel at the labour involved, they, in fact, entailed less work than if the rock had had to be quarried elsewhere and transported to the chosen site.

The Kailasa temple at Ellora is intended to be an architectural replica of the sacred Mount Kailasa—Siva's eternal home. The temple is obviously dedicated to Siva, whose

Colour Plate
15. An interesting Tibetan bronze censer in the form of a deity, wearing dharmapala ornaments and in the vajrahumkara. Probably Samantabhadra. 19th century. Ht. 16 cm.

lingam is enshrined in the innermost sanctuary. Some of the reliefs in the temple recall earlier reliefs from Amaravati, while figures of Siva and Paravati, carved with elongated form, are similar, stylistically, to some forms of deities at Mamallapuram. The sculpture here is essentially part of the architecture but can still be reviewed as sculpture.

75. Seated stone figure of a Jain tirthankara, probably Mahavira. Gujerat. 15th century. Ht. 20 cm.

The sculptures of Mysore are, in a way, a compromise between the Dravidian and Indo-Aryan artistic schools. The result is very original and separate and can be easily distinguished from the sculpture of other parts of India.

Executed during the Hoysala dynasty (A.D. 1050 to 1300) these sculptures are carved in a very fine-grained chloritic

Colour Plate
16. Large Thang-ka painting of the wheel of life—bhavacakramudra. Tibet. 19th century. Ht. 215 cm.

schist which, when quarried, is soft, but hardens when exposed to the air. The sculptures, mainly stele, can often come the way of collectors. As mentioned above, it is a distinctive style and reminds one not of stone sculpture but more of an enlargement of a carving in sandalwood or ivory. The figures are rigid, almost stereotyped, and highly stylised, with an over-burdening of ornamentation. The deities wear highly ornate headdresses.

The Pallava rulers of Kanchi were the dominant power in the South in the 7th century. The Vengi school in its later phase adapted and continued by the Pallava sculptors.

The Pallava style itself is expressed in tall and slender figures. The arms, long, slim—almost cylindrical—emphasise the elongation of the figure, which shows greater vitality than the early Vengi figures. Female forms are slim, with narrow waists and small shoulders. The breasts are well rounded, but smaller than those of the Vengi figures. They wear fewer ornaments and garments. The male figure is heavier, with broad shoulders, supported on an elongated torso. Less attention is paid to the expression of emotions through facial movement, and more to pose and gesture. These descriptions apply both to human and divine forms.

The cave shrines and sculpture of Mahavalipuram reflect the final stage in the classical ideas of the South.

Probably the greatest phase of Dravidian sculpture, both in stone and bronze, was under the Cholas. One of the greatest architectural achievements, from the point of view of sheer size, was realised during the reign of the Chola king Rajaraja the Great (King of Kings). In A.D. 1000 he erected a temple to the god Siva at Tanjore. This temple, the Rajrajesvara, was 180 feet long and had a tower which rose 190 feet into the air The height was achieved by a pyramidical structure, on a base 50 feet square. The top of the spire was capped by a large stone, weighing 80 tons! This, surely, can be ranked amongst the greatest of megalithic achievements. It required a ramp four miles long to get the stone into position, a gradient of approximately one in 35 feet. This I think, gives some idea of the determination of both Chola artists and technicians in the realisation of perfection.

The Chola style was not limited to the South but was exported and had a powerful influence on the contemporary architecture of South-East Asia. The appearance of the stone sculpture was similar to the metal images. The figures were carved tall and slender, with long faces.

As mentioned in the earlier chapter on metal sculpture, the State of Vijayanagar was one of fabulous wealth, learning and art. Its temples were covered with fine sculpture, the style of which was one of fantastic baroque ornaments and figures. The figures were sharply carved in chlorite, that was afterwards polished. The compositions were delicate and intricate. The stone was worked with such mastery that the artist could not resist embellishing the piece with every detail.

Unfortunately, after Vijayanagar was conquered by the Mohammedan invaders in 1565, the victors spent a whole year in systematically destroying the city. All that was left was rubble. However, the Vijayanagar style did not die. It continued in South India long after the city had fallen. The 17th century temple at Srirangam preserves fine examples of columns in the form of rearing horsemen, each standing approximately 9 feet high.

The Dravidian style continued into the Nayak dynasty, who had their capital at Madura. The sculpture of this period was stereotyped, adhering to the rigid canons and giving little character to the almost mass-produced works. However, they are of interest to the collector.

In addition to the South Indian stone carvings, the collector will be able to obtain many fine wood sculptures. Mainly reliefs, in the form of panels, they were made in the 17th to the 18th century and depict religious scenes from the Ramayana and Mahabarata, and images of deities. Some are architectural fragments.

Ceylon

Buddhism was introduced into Ceylon in the reign of Devanam Piyatissa (247 to 207 B.C.) by the missionary activities of the son of the Emperor Asoka.

There has always been a very close connection between Ceylon and India. The artistic influence of the latter lasted until the 13th century but the relationship was not always friendly. Many times during Ceylon's colourful history it had to contend with attacks and incursions from the Tamils of South India. Anuradhapura was taken in the 8th century and Polonnaruwa fell in the 15th century. Buddhism has remained, however, and is a living religion in the country.

An idea of the great wealth of the early buildings can be seen in the ruins of Lohapasada at Anuradhapura, built by King Gamani. This is a maze of 1,600 granite pillars. An ancient text describes the building as a royal monastery. The superstructure was of wood, roofed with copper sheets, with fittings in ivory and jewels.

A number of Singhalese sculptures of the Buddha in dolo-

76. Volcanic stone sculpture of Nairrta. From Central Java. 9th–10th century A.D. Ht. 87·5 cm.

mite, of the 2nd to 3rd century, recalls an old relationship with Amaravati. Comparison of the Hinayana Buddhas with those of Amaravati will show the source of inspiration of the Singhalese figures. The drapery of the Hinayana figures is completely in the Amaravati style, with garments represented by ridges and incised lines. They also have the large billowing fold at the bottom, in the south-eastern Indian style. These images have a sort of hieratic quality, caused by their rigid pose and massive proportions. They seem to have a grandeur which reminds one of the early figures of Buddha at Mathura. The seated Buddha images of the early period have a fine abstract quality of form and an air of serenity and dignity.

The reliefs of Dvarapalas, or gate guardians, in the form of nagas, are popular in the early Anuradhapura sculptures and recall Amaravati work.

Carvings in the Pallava style at Isurumuniyavihar, near

Anuradhapura, testify to the continued relationship with south-eastern India. It is thought that the sculptures, on a rock face, date to the period immediately preceding the retreat from Anuradhapura in the 8th century. The sculpture of Polonnaruwa continues the artistic tradition founded at Anuradhapura. The reign of Parakrama Bahu I (1164—1197) marks the period of great artistic activity at the site. The colossal standing figures are masterpieces of their style.

Hindu temples were also erected and some have been uncovered in the jungles of Polonnaruwa. These date to the period of the Chola occupation in the 11th century, but were desecrated in the 13th century by Parakrama Bahu II. The style is the same as South Indian Chola. Sculpture continued to be made after the fall of Polonnaruwa in the 13th century, but the forms and techniques are debased.

Nepal and Tibet

Sculpture was produced in Nepal and Tibet but is much rarer than the metal icons. The earlier examples in Nepal are closely connected with the Pala styles of Eastern India. Later sculptures were also made in the Pala style, but with strong Mongolian influence. Both Buddhist and Hindu subjects were depicted.

In Tibet, sculptures, other than metal, are very rare but, when they occur, are made in the same tradition, and for the same purpose, as their metal counterparts.

Purchasing Sculpture

Before leaving the subject of sculpture, a word or two about purchasing. When buying sculpture, take great care and examine it carefully for evidence of restoration and repairs. Scrutinise its surface. Has it been damaged? Have scars or chips been filled in? Have the features or decoration been re-cut? These are the questions one ought to ask oneself. There are many tricks employed by unscrupulous people and the unsuspecting collector can be taken in. Scars and holes can be filled in with wax or plaster. A little probing and careful examination, however, should reveal this. Only experience, however, will tell one if the sculpture has been re-cut, but this is rarely done, as it, in itself, requires great skill. More often one finds the copy or forgery. The former is an actual sculpture, but a copy of an earlier school. Some of these are being produced by dealers in India but I have not met many in this country. Perhaps they are too heavy to ship out! Whereas the copy is unlikely to deceive, a good composition forgery can easily fool, if one is not on guard. These are sometimes cast in stone dust, or even cement, from a mould made from an original piece. The result is extremely effective but close scrutiny will often reveal air bubbles and blurred edges, when the original has been sharply carved. So be on the look-out —all that glitters is not gold.

INDIAN PAINTING

Indian Miniatures Pre Mughal

Apart from architecture, which is outside the scope of this book, painting is the third great art form of India. For the purpose of this account we shall examine briefly the early mural schools, which flourished at Ajanta and other places in India, and concentrate on the late Gujerati, the Mughal and the Hindu schools, of which the collector will be able to find many beautiful and wonderful examples. The early styles, although of great artistic merit, are of only historical interest to the collector, as they were mainly executed as murals. The most impressive of these early paintings can be seen at Ajanta. Here, in the caves, frescoes were painted from the Satavahana period to later times. Except for a few minor historical scenes the subjects are all Buddhist. As the early sculptors tended to express the lives of the Buddha (Jatakas) three-dimensionally in stone, so the painters tried to express the same themes two-dimensionally as frescoes. Buddhism is essentially a graphic religion and a source of artistic inspiration. This can be seen clearly in the art of Tibet. To the Buddhist, art was not meant purely to decorate and beautify, but mainly to teach and inspire the devotee at places of worship. As India was the birth place of Buddhism, so we can assume that it was also the birth place of Buddhist art.

The rock-cut temples of Ajanta and Hyderabad (first discovered in 1819) preserve frescoes which date approximately from the 1st century A.D. to the 7th century A.D., an extremely valuable continuous series of paintings (with the exception of a small gap), ranging over six centuries.

The earlier works bear some resemblance to the sculptures of Amaravati, Bharhut and Sanchi, a fact which shows that here we have no primitive beginning, but a mature art form, indicating that there must have been many earlier paintings at other sites, which, alas, have been lost to us.

The composition of these scenes is masterful. The paintings

are simple, but bold, with vigorous outlines. The treatment of the figures is delicate and executed with great skill. The hands are extremely expressive. The style continues, with little change, until the 7th century.

Other paintings of the early Buddhist school can be found at Bagh in Gwalior and Sigiriya in Ceylon.

Although there are few surviving examples of wall painting, the tradition continued and did not die out until the 12th century A.D. The temples and palaces of Central and Northern India, however, had murals painted in the 16th, 17th and 18th centuries, but in a different style.

In order to appreciate these paintings they must be seen first-hand in India. While it is quite difficult for the majority of people to do this, they can easily afford to appreciate later forms of Indian art, either by owning examples themselves or by viewing them in museums.

The Chinese critic, Teng Ch'un, wrote in the 11th century that the monks of Nalanda in Bihar 'painted pictures of Buddhas and Bodhisattvas on the linen of the west'. The style of Bengal during the Pala period seems to be connected with that of Nepal and Tibet, and even Central Asia. None of the linen pictures have been found but Pala paintings are preserved on palm-leaf manuscripts of the 11th and 12th centuries A.D. These are often delicately painted but are principally book illustrations and are rather stereotyped.

Dhiman and Bitpalo are mentioned by Tibetan historians as founding the Pala school of painting. In 1299 the Moslems invaded Bengal and the Pala style died out.

In Gujerat, too, miniatures were painted on manuscripts, the earliest of which date to the 11th to 12th centuries A.D. These paintings are highly stylised. The figures have very sharp features, pointed noses, double chins and eyes which project outwards from the face. The colouring is predominantly red and yellow, with some blue. Unlike the Pala manuscripts their themes are mainly derived from Jain texts.

The style persisted until the 16th century, when many practitioners of the art were employed under Persian masters at the courts of the Mughal rulers, thus helping to formulate a new style.

The charm of the Gujerati school is mainly in its naïve approach. Paper was introduced in the 14th century and allowed the artist greater space for the expansion of his themes. There are many varied and interesting illustrations in the Gujerati style to attract the collector. Most of the illustrations appear in just a small area of the leaf.

Local variations of the style occurred when it spread to centres in Central and Northern India.

Although Gujerat was ruled by Moslem sultans from the 14th to the 16th centuries, they took little interest in its art form, preferring to import illustrated manuscripts from Persia. A favourite subject for illustration was the Kalpasutra.

During the late 15th century the style became more ornate. The painting was sometimes encircled, along with the text (which might be executed in gold), by a floral border.

Mughal

Much has been said up to now of the destruction of artistic works caused by the Moslem invasion of India—but it was not all destruction. The invaders brought with them a culture, which, although different from the indigenous, in many ways enhanced the later art forms of India, especially painting. The Mughal emperors brought to their court from Persia, painters versed in the art of miniature painting. These painters employed local artists in their ateliers, who were proficient in the Gujerati style. Soon a new school of painting was born— the Mughal school, which ranks amongst the greatest in Asia.

Indian miniatures have been known in the West since the 16th century. Rembrandt was familiar with them and made some free copies of them. In the 18th century large private collections were made by Richard Johnson and Sir Gore Ouseley.

The Emperor Akbar (1556 to 1605) can be said to have been the founder of the Mughal school. It was under his personal supervision that the court studios grew up, staffed with local artists under the direction of Mir Sayyid Ali and Abdas Samaad, two master painters from Persia, who had come to India with Akbar's father, Humayan. Of the local artists, among others we know the names of Basawan, Daswanth and Kesadosa. Some accounts say that there were over a hundred artists working in the capital.

Akbar was a great patron of the arts and commissioned many large projects. The Hamza Namah is now known to have been painted during his reign. Started about 1567, it was completed in 1582. Consisting of 1,400 paintings on linen, it was previously thought to have been painted during the reign of Humayan. Artists came to Akbar's court from all over India to work on the project.

The painting of this early work shows a very strong Persian

influence but later this was modified under the influence of both Hindu and European ideas.

The average size of Indian miniatures of the 16th century is about 12 inches by 8 inches. In technique they resemble the illustrations in European medieval manuscripts.

Unlike most of the art previously described, the Mughal paintings were not inspired by religion. The Koran specifically states that whosoever made a representation of a figure— whether human or animal, would give it his soul on the Day of Judgment. Although this was originally meant to cover representations of figures of all kinds, and was adhered to during early times, it was later only applied to buildings used for religious purposes.

Subjects of Mughal paintings included scenes from actual life, historical incidents, portraits, etc. Akbar specially commissioned many Hindu epics and other works to be illustrated for his library.

The earliest pictures, sometimes described as Indo-Persian, were painted in reds, blues and golds—a kaleidoscope of colours. The blues were ground from lapis lazuli. Gold leaf was frequently used on back-grounds and for the designs and accessories of costumes. The painting is fine and delicate and is closely related to the Persian style.

The true Mughal is quite different. It is freer and more realistic than the earlier works. The introduction of fine line shading is probably the result of European influence. The backgrounds are more natural. The Mughal painters had a unique sense of perspective and many attempts were made at foreshortening.

The care that the Mughal artists lavished on their works can be seen in the trouble they took in the choosing and preparation of their materials. Like the artists of the West they made most of their own pigments, many to their personal formulas. Paper was chosen from three kinds: bhansi, made from bamboo, tataha, from jute, and tulat, from cotton—while a fourth variety, sunni, made from flax, was used occasionally.

The paper, when selected, was burnished with an agate pebble to give it a uniform enamel-like surface. For separate works, two pieces were used, and stuck together, back to back, while single sheets were used for book illustration.

The outlines were always made first in Indian red, which could be easily removed, as it was not mixed with binding agents. After being primed with semi-transparent white, this outline was blacked in with lamp black. The colours were then painted in, the details being added last. Brushes were made of squirrel, monkey or camel hair. The pigments, which were made from natural substances, were applied with water, mixed with binding agents, such as gum, sugar or glue. Often more than one artist was employed on the production of a picture. One would specialise on the drawing of the outline, another on the main subject and, sometimes, yet another on the background. As in European schools, apprentices worked under the direction of masters, painting in minor areas, but the resulting work was always known by the master's name. The main panel of an Indian miniature is known as the taswir; the border as hashia. The mounting was not the work of the artist, but of another individual, a specialist in his field. There is usually a buffer area between the panel and the border, a band of solid colour, sometimes decorated with flowers, etc. The hashia was commonly speckled with gold leaf. This mounting technique is common to both the Mughal and the Hindu schools.

Akbar's son, Jehangir (1605–1627) continued his father's interest in painting. It was during Jehangir's reign that the flower of Mughal painting bloomed. He inherited his father's studios, commissioned many works and formed collections, both of contemporary and early paintings. These were mounted in uniform size in large albums. Elaborate floral borders seem to have been specially developed by Jehangir's court ateliers, possibly for the purpose of enhancing the overall appearance of the royal albums.

During Jehangir's reign the style became more naturalistic. The Persian idea of bird's-eye perspective was replaced by the popular side view of the Rajput style. Jehangir commissioned botanical and zoological studies. These beautiful and delicate paintings are masterpieces of Mughal art. Other subjects popular at the time include illustrations of historical works, romances, hunting scenes and group portraits. Single portraits, too, were very popular and many are works of sheer genius. Amusing paintings of Europeans, etc., and copies of occidental paintings were also executed. European art had a definite effect on the art of the Mughal court. The European influence can be seen in the introduction of faint line shading, giving a quality of depth to the otherwise flat style.

There is a recorded instance of an artist working in India, who had actually studied under Italian masters in Rome in the early 17th century. Muhammad Zaman, a Persian artist,

138

studied in Rome, became a Christian and changed his name to Paolo Zaman. He was not allowed back to Persia and obtained asylum under Shah Jehan in India, where he worked as a painter. At least three paintings in the European style in the British Museum are thought to be by him.

During the reign of Shah Jehan (1628–1658) a technique known as Siyahi Kalam (line drawings with just a touch of colour) became very fashionable in portraiture.

The flower of Mughal painting begins to wilt a little during this period but does not completely die for nearly 200 years. Portraiture in the Mughal court was extremely popular and the emperors had their portraits painted, often many copies being made of one painting, either by the same artist or by his assistant. Royal personages are nearly always shown with a halo of gold round their heads. The portraits are true to life and drawn with fine and delicate lines.

The figure is usually shown in profile, the garments richly painted in mosaic colouring, enhanced with gold. When diaphanous robes were painted, the limbs were shown clearly beneath the folds. Back-grounds were usually plain, painted in tinted colours, though occasionally dark colours were used. The artist relied on the colouring and delicate line drawings for effect.

The stiffness of Mughal portraits is relieved somewhat by the soft natural treatment of the hands, which, in the case of men, are often shown resting on the sword-hilt or holding a flower. The Mughals were very fond of nature and it was not unmanly to be portrayed like this. The figure was usually shown standing on a grass patch, with flowers, or on a terrace. Original portraits are full of character and can usually be distinguished from the later stereotyped copies.

Portraits were not only made of contemporary kings and courtiers, saints and soldiers, but also of kings and great personages of the past. It is occasionally possible to come across portraits of three successive emperors, all seated together.

Mughal painting declined under the Emperor Aurangzeb (1658–1708), as this despotic ruler took no interest in the work of the painters. Paintings, however, continued to be made, though the subjects were mainly court, hunting and war scenes, and portraits.

It was due to this lack of patronage that artists began to move elsewhere in search of work. They found it in the courts of the Rajasthani Rajahs and Punjab hill states. A new vigorous school developed, free of the limitations of the Mughal court, illustrating such dynamic works as the Hindu epics.

In the 18th century Mughal painting entered a new phase. From the time of Akbar until the death of Shah Jehan, painting was a royal art, produced for emperors, princes and the nobility, but by the 18th century, painting had grown popular with the merchant classes and people of similar status, whose growing demands for paintings had to be met.

At court, favoured subjects changed; musicians and dancing girls were all the rage. Delhi was in an era of imperial pleasure. Paintings of dancing girls, courtesans, zenana scenes, love scenes, dance parties and musical scenes were very popular. The change of subject necessitated, also, a variation in style. The paintings of this period are different and in no way compare with the work commissioned under Jehangir and Akbar, but they are beautiful and delicate, executed with a strong sense of composition and colour, and are in a class of their own. During this period we see a spread of Mughal artists from the capital to provincial centres, where they were encouraged by noble and wealthy patrons.

Vigorous styles of painting grew up at Murshidabad, Patna and Farrukhabad. Their individuality is marked both by subtle differences in style and by a preference for warm colours. Popular scenes were illustrations of musical themes—raga malas—hunting scenes, portraits, and group portraits of rulers with their courtiers.

The sack of Delhi in 1739 by Nadir Sha, and continued unrest, made many more artists leave the capital.

At Faizabad the Nawabs of Oudh encouraged the arts. Paintings were executed in brilliant colours and intricate compositions.

As mentioned before, a popular Mughal school had grown up to cater for the taste of the merchant classes for miniature paintings. These popular works were executed in the Mughal style, preference being given to literary subjects and portrait studies. Though not executed by the great court painters, they are attractive, interesting, and well worth collecting.

Paintings in regional styles were made at Lucknow. These were similar to those of Delhi but were not of the same quality. The technique differed, with a preference for almost pure water colours, while white was often used for the background. The style of Patna is cruder than that of Delhi. The drawing is fine but the over-all effect is hard.

In the Deccan the local paintings that developed were small, almost sub-miniature in style. Apart from this they are similar to those of Delhi, but are richer in colour and embellished in gold. The style was strongly influenced by the earlier non-Mughal traditions and also by Western influence from Portuguese Goa.

Provincial Mughal paintings continued to be produced up to the first quarter of the 19th century. The Company School developed as a branch of the Mughal school. The British, especially in Bengal and Madras, commissioned local artists to paint pictures of every-day life. These included landscapes, birds and animals, trades, transport, costumes, and even paintings of their houses and gardens. The Indian artists adapted themselves to the wishes of their new patrons, both in colour and technique. Many of the pictures are, in fact, reminiscent of British water colours of the period. Artistically they are not as good as those of the provincial school. However, they are of interest as records of contemporary life. A later variation of this school is to be found in paintings of similar themes on mica.

Rajasthan & Central India

The paintings of Central India and Rajasthan run parallel to and contemporary with the Mughal paintings.

The style is unique. The colours of the 16th and early 17th century paintings were brilliant and contrasted strongly with Mughal paintings. They were often distorted and the compositions were stark. Later, as Mughal painting was appreciated over a wider area, the Rajasthani school adapted some of the techniques, which tended to soften the effects. This happened, in particular, in Colah, Marwar, Kishangarh and Bikanen.

In addition to portraits, raga malas and scenes from every-day life, the themes for many of the Rajasthani and Central Indian paintings were derived from mythological and religious works. Compared with the Mughal school, the Hindu paintings are not realistic, but are to a certain extent stylised, and a continuation of the indigenous tradition, changed and influenced by the Indo-Persian ideals. The technique for the preparation and painting of the picture was, however, the same as the Mughal. It is the style and colouring that are different.

In some cases, silver and gold primings were used to great effect, giving the picture a luminous quality. The gold was used in pictures which represented two-lighting effects, such as moonlight and firelight, together with clever techniques

77. Mughal painting (Delhi). About 1820. A nautch party performing in a European mansion. Ht. 28 cm.

which gave a luminous effect to the shadows. Silver was utilised for the effect of still water.

Themes were drawn from the Puranas, which told about the exploits of Indian kings and heroes. Paintings of Krishna were very popular.

The centre of the early Rajasthani school seems to have been at Mewar. Other local styles can be recognised, which developed in the 17th century, at Bundi, Marwar, Narsingarh, etc. The heyday of the Rajasthani school was the 17th century. Later work became more and more influenced by the Mughal school. The small State of Kishanagarh produced a short but brilliant period of painting between A.D. 1735 and 1755.

The 18th and early 19th centuries saw the production of large numbers of paintings from the courts of the Rajput princes and nobles. Hundreds of artists were employed for the production of paintings of court scenes, portraits, hunting scenes, music parties, etc. Some very fine paintings of elephants were produced at Bundi.

Radical changes to Western ideas of Indian painting were

142

78. Raja Umed Singh of Kotah (1771–1819), shooting tigers. Kotah, Rajasthan. About 1790. Ht. 32·5 cm.

made by the art historian, A. K. Coomaraswamy in his book 'Rajput Painting', published in 1916. Although entitled 'Rajput Painting', his book dealt principally with the art of the Punjab hills. His classification of the Hindu school into two groups, Jammu and Kangra, has been superseded, and we can now classify paintings into many regional styles.

Punjab Hills

The hill states form two main groups: the western (Jammu), including Jammu itself and Basohli; and the eastern group (Kangra), including Kangra itself, Guler, Chamba and the Kulu Valley. There are really three main styles.

The constant change in the style of painting of the Punjab hills are due directly to the changes in the political relationships between the states, and also to contact with the style of the Mughal court. These influences acted as stimuli, causing constant change and development. Though there may be changes and differences between the states, they are all recognisable as a group.

It is thought that the first Raja to form an atelier in the hills was Raja Kirpal Pal of Basohli (1678–1694). Previous to this we have no evidence of book illustrations or miniatures of any kind being made in the Hills. The style of Basohli became the principal one of the Hills, influencing all other states.

Many of the artists of the atelier had left the court of Aurangzeb and found a patron in Kirpal Pal. The school that grew up in Basohli was therefore strongly influenced by the Mughal style. The Basohli style, which seems to have been the common one of the Jammu group of states, is notable for its strong lines and daring use of hot colours. The backgrounds contain large areas of a single colour, such as yellow, red, orange (as the fruit) and green, etc. The figures appear to be exaggerated, almost stylised. Both men and women are drawn with sloping foreheads and large eyes and the painting is flat, with little attention paid to perspective.

The zenith of Basohli painting was reached between 1675 and 1740. As a style it is most distinctive and once seen can never be forgotten. There are numerous sub-styles. In some cases the treatment of hands and legs of standing figures is similar to that of ancient Egyptian frescoes.

The style seems to have toned down by 1730 and was further dampened and naturalised by a new influx of Mughal artists, who had left Delhi after it was sacked in 1739. This subdued version of the Basohli style, known as the 'pre-Kangra', spread throughout the hill states and prevailed until 1765. The Basohli style, however, continued to be an important force and was still used in Chamba as late as 1770.

Many of the Mughal artists who fled to the Hills were instrumental in helping to form the new style of Guler. There they worked on illustrating the Hindu epics, especially the Krishna legend, taking full advantage of the fresh new atmosphere which the Mughal court had lacked. Some of the best paintings in the style are the very fine portraits of Govardhan Chand, ruler of Guler, made during the period 1745 to 1770. This style led to the development of the true Kangra school. This generic term is applied to all paintings in the style—not just those painted at Kangra. It remained a major style from about 1770 to 1805, although it continued in a decadent form under the Sikh rulers well into the 19th century. For the first decade it retained many elements derived from the Guler paintings. Later it became repetitive in execution, sentimental

79. Basohli painting, Punjab Hills, *circa* 1680. 'The Deceitful Heroine', a lady blames the cat for scratches inflicted by her secret lover. Ht. 23 cm.

and facile. The females shown are of two main facial types. The Bhagavata type—so-called because it first appears in a series of illustrations of the Bhagavata Purana—is delicate and small, round, with rounded chin, small nose and finely painted hair. The other, 'standard type' of face, has a mass of black hair, narrow slanting eyes, pointed chin and a straight nose, the line of which continues upwards to the forehead.

The painting of women in Kangra was in true romantic spirit. Kangra painting contrasts strongly with that of Basohli, in that it is more delicate and refined, but the passionate quality of the Basohli paintings is sacrificed at the expense of this refinement.

In India the lover is often symbolised as a woman; the beloved as a man. This is why many of the scenes depicted in the miniatures show women enflamed by passion, visiting their lovers or waiting in secret meeting places. It is the female quality to love, rather than be loved, which is stressed in the paintings. The Ragamalas were, in a way, musical love poems, or 'garlands of music'. The illustrations depicted the various musical modes, Raga or Ragini, as if they were a prince or a lady.

Many paintings of the Hindu schools were executed as a proof of devotion. Just as the saying of the sacred names of Rama or Krishna would help the devotee to ensure his ultimate bliss, so the illustrating of the epics of Rama and Krishna was

80. Sudama approaching the Golden City of Krishna. North India (Garhwal, Punjab Hills). About A.D. 1785.

thought to be a devotional act and an offering to God. It was therefore important for the sponsor to commission the best possible illustrations he could afford, for in this way his gesture would be more effective.

It is interesting to reflect on the cost of these miniature paintings, both Mughal and Rajput, in comparison with the prices paid today. With the exception of a very short period they have always been highly valued. In 1641 a Spanish priest, Father Sebastian Manrique, who was in Agra at that time, valued the imperial library, which contained approximately 24,000 volumes, at $3,500,000, an average of about $150 a volume—in 1641!

Although it is possible to describe the drawing, the colouring, the techniques of painting, and the style, there is no substitute for experience, and the collector should view as many Indian miniatures as possible, to acquaint himself with the numerous variations and styles. This is the only really reliable way to appreciate the technique and to be able to distinguish the different schools and periods. Much can be learned from a book but, in the end, experience gained from actually seeing paintings is all-important.

Folk Paintings

In addition to the classical schools of painting there existed, and still exist, folk schools. These paintings are very interesting as they show a continuity in style not found in the classical works.

Probably the best known of these folk paintings are those of Kalighat, made near the Kalighat Temple, Calcutta. These paintings, the subject of many books and articles, were made from the 19th century and were mass-produced for sale to pilgrims. The subjects were many and varied, ranging from the pictures of Hindu gods and goddesses, Kali, Siva, Brahma and Ganesha, to the various incarnations of Vishnu, including Krishna. Other subjects reflected the local life around the temple.

Kali is the patroness of prostitutes, of which the area around the temple has a large population, like other great centres of pilgrimage in India, and these women were a popular subject for the artists. These paintings are free and unbound by convention. The colours are vivid and the lines free-flowing and decisive. Although a city suburb, the paintings of Kalighat contain many Bengali village elements. The bright colours, the simplified form and flowing lines, combined with Western culture, such as the use of shading and water-colour technique, and also the materials—the factory-produced paper.

When 'discovered' in the 1920s, it created quite a stir among the art critics, who compared the paintings to the Impressionist and Cubist, etc.

All this is by the way—but it is, perhaps, interesting to note that there is a painting in the Archer Collection, London, of a hand holding shrimps, which is almost certainly the model (or one copy of the theme) which the French painter, Fernand Leger, used for his painting of 'Hand with Water Syphon'.

An art form which has not long been recognised, but which has been going for centuries, is the folk art of Orissa, which has its centre near the Jaganath Temple in Puri. These paintings were produced on a prepared cotton cloth in yellows, reds and browns, with some blue and green. They are still produced in the same technique, but on paper.

The subjects of the pictures revolve around Jaganath (another name for Krishna), the commonest being Jaganath with his brother, Balabhadra, and his sister, Subhadra. Highly stylised, they are painted in black, white and yellow, almost like children's paintings, with large eyes and crescent-shaped mouths. Sometimes the figures have no arms or legs. At other times Jaganath is shown as Krishna, with Radha. Like the Kalighat paintings they were made to be sold to pilgrims visiting the Jaganath Temple.

There are many other forms of folk art, which, apart from the main styles described here, are outside the scope of this book. Perhaps the most interesting of folk styles can be found in the Patas of the Santal Parganas, on the Bihar/Bengal border. These paintings are about one foot wide and ten or more feet long. They were painted by Chitrakars—Hindu painters/entertainers, who used the scrolls, when they visited villages, to illustrate the stories they told. For this reason the Patas have a short life and when found are in bad condition. When they were thought to be too bad for further use, the Chitrakars painted another, either from memory, or by copying the old one. Six main subjects were illustrated: the story of the Santals, the Santal life, Santal clans, the Kingdom of Death, the Krishna legend, and a god who rules tigers. The pictures, which are painted on a single flat plane, have a dynamic quality of line and colour, and a naïve charm.

Tibet and Nepal

The Thang-ka paintings of Tibet and Nepal are religious works and meant for teaching, rather than for decoration, although many that hung in the Lamasaries were of great beauty. Thang-kas were also hung on the walls of homes and carried in religious processions. Although the style is ancient and the paintings may look extremely old, in fact many may not be older than the 17th century. Thang-kas belonging to travelling monks tend to 'age' quickly, as they are rolled and unrolled many times. Another illusion of age is created by the dark colour, the film caused by the smoke of butter lamps. Thang-kas are sometimes so heavily impregnated with this soot that they retain a strong smell.

Closely related in style to the Pala paintings of Bengal, they were, in fact, executed in the technique of mural painting.

148

Produced on cotton or canvas, the ground was prepared in the same way as murals, and then painted in tempora.

The ancestor of the Thang-ka can probably be seen in the temple banners of Chiu-tzu, Central Asia, which date to about the 8th century.

81. Rajasthan painting of a nobleman with attendants. 18th century. Ht. 39 cm.

The technique of Thang-ka painting is interesting. The ground was first prepared by stretching the cloth over a wooden frame. A mixture of lime plaster, and flour, sometimes with added glue, was then spread over its surface. When dry this was burnished with a polished stone.

The outline was drawn with charcoal, or sometimes produced from a stencil plate. This was a sheet of paper, with the motif perforated with pin-holes, through which charcoal dust was sifted. The charcoal outline was then fixed in with Indian ink. Colours, which were simply mixed with hot, thin glue, were imported from China and India. The painting was not varnished and was liable to be attacked by damp. For this reason, therefore, Thang-kas must not be kept in a damp atmosphere. When finished, the panel was mounted on a silk or brocade banner.

The subjects of the Thang-ka were naturally religious, illustrating the Buddhas and other deities of the Tibetan Buddhist Pantheon. Tibetanised Hindu gods were also included, such as Ganesha and Kubera.

Thang-ka paintings can be separated into several types: those depicting manifestations of deities; Mandalas, ritual diagrams; Tshog-shing, depicting assemblies of deities; and Bhavacakramudra, the Wheel of Life.

Mandalas were used by Lamas in special rituals, invoking deities to grant Siddhi—superhuman powers. These charts are divided into sections, containing various deities. In order to receive the deity, the Thang-ka is drawn in geometrical sections, with divinities placed at key positions, according to the magical pattern. Instructions for producing the various kinds of Mandalas are included in the twenty-two volumes of the Tantra.

Tshog-shing (or Assembly Tree of the Gods) are paintings of the numerous deities of the Pantheon, assembled together, in order of rank. The central figure is usually Gautama, or Tsong-kha-pa. Deities from the whole of the Pantheon are depicted on these pictures, including the Buddhas, Bodhisattvas, Dharmapala, Yi-dam, feminine deities, witches, arhats, great magicians, etc.

The Wheel of Life, or Bhavacakramudra, is intended to represent the Samsara, the eternal cycle of life and re-birth. The Wheel is divided into sections to illustrate the Conditions of Existence. (For detailed description, see Waddell's 'Lamaism', p. 105.)

Tibetan painting is a subtle blend of Chinese and Indian

elements. The technique of depicting flowers and trees, mountains, clouds and rivers, owes its inspiration to Chinese art forms. The painting shows delicate detail, indicating the Tibetan artist's close observation of nature, but only the essential details are included. Chinese influence can also be seen in the treatment of visions, or dreams, which the Tibetan artist shows as a transparent mist floating in space.

Indian influence is shown in the treatment of the figures and costumes and the arrangement of the deities in the compositions. The idea of showing the importance of the central figure by its large size, in comparison with the others, may also have been derived from India.

Purchasing

When buying paintings it is not so much the danger of forgeries that has to be borne in mind, but of acquiring retouched paintings and later copies of earlier works. Here, it is the collector who is his own worst enemy. Through lack of experience, or simply through his over-enthusiastic wish to own an older or better painting, he might be tempted to date paintings older than they may be, or attribute them to rare schools. Only a good knowledge of painting styles, gained by viewing as many pictures as possible in museums and private collections, will help. With regard to re-touched paintings, only close examination will reveal if this has been done. Forgeries do exist, but they are rare.

Glossary of gods and goddesses and mythological personages
Hindu—Jain—Buddhist including Tibet
and Notes on Identification

Abhinandana—A Tirthankara.
Adibuddha—Primordial Buddha. Creator of the Universe. (T) Image has usnisa, long lobed ears, urna and wears bodhisattva ornaments and costume.
Aditi—Wife of Kasyapa.
Aditya—Son of Aditi.
Agni—Fire God (Vedic). Vahana—Ram.
Airavata—Elephant. Vehicle of Indra.
Aiyanar—Commander of Heavenly Hosts
Ajitanatha—A Tirthankara.
Amama—A Tirthankara.
Amitabha—Dhyanibuddha. Vahana—Peacock. Image (T) has

hands in dhyana mudra holding patra.

Ananthanatha—A Tirthankara.

Anantavirya—A Tirthankara.

Apsaras—Celestial Nymphs.

Aruna—Charioteer of Sun.

Asura—Enemy of the Gods. Demon.

Atisa—Hindu Priest. Founded Ka-dam-pa sect in Tibet. Image (T), wears monastic robes, peaked cap. Hands in dhamacakra mudra. His symbol is a caitya.

Avalokitesvara—God of Mercy. Dhyanibodhisattva. Image (T). Symbols mala and padma. Mudra—Namaskara. Seated or standing. Tantric form has four heads and twenty-four arms.

Balakrishna—Krishna dancing with ball of butter (image).

Balarama—Brother of Krishna. Symbol—Hala (plough).

Bhadrajina—A Tirthankara.

Bodhisattva—One who has forsaken Nirvana in order to intercede on behalf of humans. (Mahayana Buddhism.)

Buddha—Gautama. One who has obtained Nirvana. Enlightened One. Founder of Buddhism. Image (T) has urna, usnisa and long lobed ears. Wears monastic ornaments without ornaments.

Brahma—One of the Hindu Trinity. The Creator. He has four heads—in images sometimes shown as four faces. Symbols: kamandalu—water vessel, mala, pustaka, srava—spoon.

Chandika—A form of Durga.

Chandra—The Moon.

Chandraprabha—A Tirthankara.

Chitragupta—A Tirthankara.

Dalai Lama—Ruler of Tibet. Incarnation of Avalokitesvara.

Dakini—Female divinities of lesser rank.

Devadatta—Arch enemy of Buddha.

Devajina—A Tirthankara.

Devaki—Mother of Krishna.

Devasruta—A Tirthankara.

Devata—Godling.

Dharmanatha—A Tirthankara.

Dharmapala—Defenders of the Law of Buddhism. In images (T) all wear dharmapala ornaments except Kubera and Sitabrahma.

Dhyanibuddhas—Spiritual Sons of Adibuddha. Images (T) have urna, usnisa, long lobed ears and the short and curly hair. Garment—monastic shawl.

Dhyanibodhisattvas—Actual creators of the Universe. Image (T) wears bodhisattva costume and ornaments. Usnisa in high chignon, sometimes a urna or third eye. Five leafed crown or headress with figure of their Spiritual Father.

Dikpala—World guardian.

Durga—Form of Devi. Image (H) has ten arms, holds symbols: cakra, trisula, shanka, agni, bow, quiver and arrow, iron rod, a bared roll, vajra, gada, parusu, precious stones, necklace of pearls. Vahana—lion.

Gajasimha—Monster, half lion half elephant.

Gandharvas—Celestial musicians.

Ganas—Attendants of Siva. Dwarfs. Demigods.

Ganesha—Son of Siva. Elephant headed. Vahana—rat. God of prudence and sagacity.

Ganga—River Goddess of the Ganges.

Garuda—Vehicle of Vishnu. Part man part bird.

Gautama Buddha—Founder of Buddhism. Image (T), dhyana asana, in the dharmacakra, dhyana and vitarka, or bhumisparsa. Symbol—patra.

Gopis—Milkmaids (Krishna legend).

Hanuman—Monkey God.

Hara—A form of Siva.

Isani—A form of Siva.

Isvara—Supreme deity.

Indra—(Vedic) Lord of Heavens. Vahana—white elephant. Symbol—vajra.

Jambhala—Yi-Dam. Image (T) wears bodhisattva costume and ornaments. Symbol—jambhara and nakula.

Jina—One of twenty-four Jain sages.

Kali—Form of Devi. Terrible manifestation.

Kalki—Avatar of Vishnu.

Kama—God of Love. Vahana—parrot.

Kamala—Lakshmi.

Kanakamuni—Manusibuddha. Image (T) left hand in dhyana mudra, right in abhaya mudra. No symbols.

Kartrikeya—God of War, second son of Siva. (see *Subrahmanya*) Vahana—peacock. Symbol—sakti.

Kasyapa—Manusibuddha. Image (T)—left hand in vitarka mudra holding robe. Right in varada mudra.

Kinnari—Half human, half bird. Celestial musicians.

Krishna—Incarnation of Vishnu. Symbol—flute.

Kshetrapala—Dikpala.

Kubera—God of Wealth. Guardian of the North. Chief Yaksha.

Kuntanatha—A Tirthankara.

Kurma—Tortoise avatar of Vishnu.

Lakshmi—Consort of Vishnu. Goddess of Wealth, Beauty and

Happiness.

Lakshman—Rama's half brother.

Lingam—Phallic symbol of Siva.

Lokapala—Dikpala.

Mahadeva—A name for Siva.

Mahesa—A name for Siva.

Makara—Mythical fish. Head of deer, legs of antelope, body and tail of fish.

Marpa—Founder of Kar-gyu-pa sect. As image (T) he wears monastic robes and holds pustaka in left hand and kapala in right.

Manjusri—Dhyanibodhisattva. In images (T) symbols— khadga, pustaka and utpala. Seated or standing in dharma-cakra mudra.

Manasa—Snake Goddess (Bengal).

Manusibuddhas—Mortal Buddhas. In images (T) they have urna, usnisa, long lobed ears, wear monastic garments, are bare headed and wear no ornaments.

Mallinatha—A Tirthankara.

Malyadeva—A Tirthankara.

Matsya—Fish avatar of Vishnu.

Matrika—Mother Goddess.

Mohini—A female form of Vishnu.

Munisuvarata—A Tirthankara.

Naga—Water spirit.

Nagini—Female water spirit.

Nagaraja—King of water spirits.

Naminatha—A Tirthankara.

Nandi—Sacred bull of Siva.

Nandisa—Demi God, attendant of Siva.

Nataraja—Siva as Lord of the Dance.

Narasimha—An avatar of Vishnu. Man/Lion.

Neminatha—Jain Tirthankara.

Nikasaya—A Tirthankara.

Nirmama—A Tirthankara.

Nisupalaka—A Tirthankara.

Padmanabha—A Tirthankara.

Padmapani—Form of Avalokitesvara. Symbols—padma and kalasa.

Padmasambhava—Founder of Lamaism. Images (T) show him seated on a lotus throne in dhyanasana, holding a vajra, a patra and kaatbanga. His two wives are shown beside him.

Pandavas—Five princes.

Parasvanatha—A Tirthankara.

Parasurama—Avatar of Vishnu.
Parivara-Devata—Dikpalas.
Parvati—Consort of Siva. (Devi, Uma, etc.) Vahana—lion.
Pedhala—A Tirthankara.
Potila—A Tirthankara.
Prajnaparamita —A Tirthankara.
Pushpadanta—A Tirthankara.
Radha—Krishna's beloved.
Rama—Hero of Ramayana. Avatar of Vishnu. Symbol—bow and arrow.
Rati—Consort of God of Love.
Sakyamuni—Manusibuddha. Image (T) in vitarka, varada, dharma, bhumisparsa or dhyana mudras. Symbol—patra.
Sakti—Consort of a God.
Samba—Krishna's son.
Sambhavanatha—A Tirthankara.
Samantabhadra—Dhyanibodhisattva. Symbol—cintamani.
Samvaranatha—A Tirthankara.
Sani—Saturn.
Santinatha—A Tirthankara.
Saraswati—Hindu Goddess also (T) female bodhisattva. Varada mudra. Vahana—swan. Symbol—vina.
Sarvabhuti—A Tirthankara.
Sati—Consort of Siva.
Satakirti—A Tirthankara.
Satrughna—Rama's half brother.
Simhananda—A form of Avalokitesvara. Images (T) seated on lion throne. Symbols—padma, khadga, kapala, trisula.
Sitalanatha—A Tirthankara.
Sitapatra—Female bodhisattva. Symbol—atapatra. Image (T) in abhaya mudra.
Siva—Member of the Hindu Trinity. The Destroyer. Symbols: parusu—axe, trisula—trident, kapala, agni. He may also carry mriga in his left upper hand.
Skanda—Son of Siva and Uma. (Kartikeya.)
Sri—Goddess of Good Fortune. Lakshmi.
Sri Devi—Female Dharmapala.
Sreyamasanatha—A Tirthankara.
Subrahmanya—Name for second son of Siva. Kartikeya (carries a cock).
Suddharma—A Tirthankara.
Sumadhi—A Tirthankara.
Sumantinantha—A Tirthankara.
Suradeva—A Tirthankara.

Surasundari—Heavenly Nymph.

Surya—Sun God.

Suparasvanatha—A Tirthankara.

Suvidhanantha—A Tirthankara.

Tara—Tibetan or buddhist goddess. *White* (thought to be incarnate Chinese wife of Srong-san-gampo). Image (T) in vitarka and varada mudras and dhyana asana. Padma on left shoulder. *Green:* (thought to be incarnate Nepalese wife of Srong-san-gampo) Image (T) in vitarka and varada mudras and in lalitasana. Utpala on left shoulder or both. Also in Blue, Red and Yellow forms.

Tirthankara—(or Tirthamkara). World Teacher (Jain) one of twenty-four.

Udayaprabhu—A Tirthankara.

Uma—Consort of Siva.

Vairocana—Dhyanibuddhas. Vahana—lion. Image (T) in dharmacakra mudra, both hands in dhyana mudra. Symbol—vajra.

Vajrapani—Dhyanibodhisattva (numerous forms).

Vajradhara—Primordial Buddha worshipped by Ge-lug-pa sect of Tibet.

Vajrasattva—Primordial Buddha worshipped by Ka-dam-pa (Red Cap Sect) of Tibet.

Vamana—Dwarf Avatar of Vishnu.

Varaha—Boar incarnation of Vishnu.

Varuna—God of Oceans. Vahana—Makara.

Vasuki—Serpent. Siva's girdle.

Vasudeva—Father of Krishna.

Vasupujya—A Tirthankara.

Vayu—God of Winds. Vahana—the deer.

Vijaya—Attendant of Vishnu.

Vijaya—A Tirthankara.

Vijaya—Wife of Yama.

Vimalanatha—A Tirthankara.

Vishnu—Member of the Hindu Trinity. Preserver. Symbols: cakra—shanka—gada—padma. Symbols are also used on other Vaishnavite deities (with the exception of gada).

Vyali—Lion with elephant trunk.

Yaksha—Tutelary deity.

Yama—God of Death. Vahana—buffalo.

Yani—Consort of Subrahmanya.

Yi-Dam—Tutelary divinities, with rank of Buddha. Pacific forms (T. Images) wear bodhisattva ornaments, and have urna and usnisa. Angry forms wear dharmapala ornaments.

Some forms wear both.

Yosodhara—A Tirthankara.

Yoni—Symbol of Shakti.

Glossary of Mudras, Hastas and Asanas
(Positions of the hands and body)

Mudras and Hastas

Abhaya—Protection. Right arm raised and slightly bent. Open palm held outwards, the fingers extended and directed upwards. Hand is level with shoulders.

Alinga (South India)—One arm is placed round the back of another figure. (Used on group figures, such as Siva and Parvati.)

Anjali—Salutation. Both arms raised fully upwards above head —palms turned up and fingers extended.
Some authorities disagree over this and equate it with the namaskara mudra.

Ardha-chandra—The palm and fingers form a crescent to hold fire. (Used on Nataraja images.)

Bhumisparsa—Witness. The right arm is pendant over right knee. The hand has all fingers stretched downwards, touching lotus throne, palm inward.

Bhutadamara—Awe-inspiring. Wrists crossed in front of chest. No symbols.

Buddhasramana—Salutation. Right hand level with head. Palm upwards, all fingers extended outwards.

Damaru—Similar to the tripataka, but palm faces inwards and is holding a drum.

Dharmachakra (-cakra)—Preaching. 'Wheel of Law'. Hands held against chest, left hand covering right.

Dhyana (Yoga)—Meditation. Hands lie in lap, one on the other, palms upwards and all fingers extended. Figure seated in padmasana or paryanka asana.

Gaja (South India)—One arm drawn across the body, as in icons of Nataraja.

Karana—Hand stretched outwards, fingers extended, but with second and third fingers pressing against palm.

Kataka—Hand partly closed, with thumb and tip of index finger almost touching, signifying hand holding attributes or stems of flowers.

Kati (South India)—One arm hangs loosely by the body, the other rests on the hip.

157

Ksepana—Hands clasped together, fingers interlocking, except for the two index fingers, which are turned downwards into a kalasa containing amrita (nectar).

Lola (South India)—Arm hangs down at side of figure in a semi-flexed position.

Namaskara—Hands held at chest, praying. (See Anjali.)

Nidrata (South India)—A sitting position, in which the body leans to one side and the weight is supported on one hand.

Suchi (South India)—Similar to Kataka.

Tarjani—Menacing. Hand clenched as fist but with index finger pointing upwards.

Tarpana—Homage. Arms raised above level of shoulders, with palms turned inwards, fingers pointing towards shoulders.

Tripataka—Hand raised above shoulder, with the palm outwards, two fingers separated and raised upwards to hold an attribute. (Used in images of Vishnu and Siva.)

Uttarbodhi—Similar to Ksepana but with tips of thumbs touching and index fingers pointing upwards.

Vajrahumkara—Similar to bhutadamara but holding Vajra and Ghanta.

Varda (or Vara)—Charity. Palm of the left hand opened outwards, with fingers pointing downwards. Arm pendant.

Vismaya—Astonishment. Forearm folded at elbow, with the palm of the hand facing the image, with fingers pointing upwards.

Vitarka—Arm bent, fingers extended upwards, except index finger, which touches tip of palm, which is turned outwards.

Vyakhyana—Exposition. Hand in similar position to abhaya mudra but with the thumb and forefinger touching. (v. vitarka)

Asanas

Alidhasana—Standing position. Stepping to the left, with right leg straight and left leg bent.

Ardhaparyankasana—Dancing pose.

Bhadrasana (Pralamabapada asana)—Both legs pendant. Figure seated in European style. Pose of Maitreya.

Dhyanasana—Meditation pose of Buddhas, etc. When seated on a lotus throne—padmasana.

Lalitasana—One leg bent in position of dhyanasana, the other pendant. (Same as sukhasana)

Maharaja-lilasana (Rajalilasana)—Position of royal pleasure. Right hand is raised and the left leg in position of a Buddha, or pendant. One hand hangs over knee, the other supports the body, which is leaning backwards.

Padmasana—Seated position. Legs crossed, with feet resting on thighs.

Pralamabapada asana—(See *Bhadrasana*)

Pratyalidhasana—Standing position. Stepping to the right, with left leg straight, right leg bent.

Sattvasana—Legs loosely locked. (Position of some Bodhisattvas.)

Sukhasana—Seated pose—one leg folded and resting on plinth, the other pendant.

Yab-yum—Seated or standing position. Union of God with Sakti.

Yogasana—Similar to padmasana but with knees slightly raised, supported by a band called yoga-patta.

Glossary of Technical Terms

Abhicharika—Horrific or ferocious manifestation.

Agni—Fire.

Agnidhirya—The god Agni's sacrificial fire.

Airavata—The elephant, vehicle of Indra. Symbol of clouds.

Amrita—Elixir of life. Divine nectar.

Ankusa—Elephant god, symbol of Tantric manifestations.

Arhat—Saint.

Archa—Cult image—Hindu.

Arti—Libation ritual to deity.

Asana—Seat. Throne.

Asana-murti—Seated image.

Ashtadhatu—Octo-alloy used for making metal icons.

Atapatra—Parasol.

Avadanas—Legends of the life and deeds of Buddha.

Avatar—Term applied to the incarnations of Vishnu in human or animal form.

Avatara—Epiphany of Vishnu.

Ayagapata—Votive tablet—Jain.

Ayudha—Weapons, etc. Symbols in hands of icons—Buddhist and Hindu.

Bandhana—Hair style—tying hair in a band.

Bhadramukha—Mask found on Hindu temple.

Bhaktas—Devotee of gods.

Bhakti—Devotion to gods.

Bharat Natya—Classical dance.

Bhavacakra mudra—Wheel of life.

Bhavan—House.

Bhiksu—Buddhist monk.

Bhoga—Artistic pleasure or enjoyment.

Bhumi—Literally, the ground on which all things are founded.

Bija—Seed.

Bodhisattva—The higher stages before full Nirvana. One who, although capable of attaining Buddha-hood, rejects it in preference to acting as helper to humanity (Mahayana Buddhism).

Bodhivriksha—Bodhi tree, under which the Buddha found enlightenment.

Brahmanas—Vedic texts.

Brahmin—Highest class of Hindu. Priestly class.

Buddhasramana—Salutation.

Caitya—Reliquary or shrine.

Camara—Fly whisk.

Candra—Moon.

Capa—Bow.

Carana—Buddha's footprint.

Cetana—Portrayal of the movement of life in Indian painting.

Chakra (Cakra)—Disc. Wheel. Emblem of the sun. Wheel of law.

Chakravala—In Hindu cosmology, the rings of mountains believed to encircle Mount Meru.

Channavira—Crossed scarves worn above the waist by early figures of fertility goddesses.

Chitra—Images in the round.

Chitra-ardha—Bas-relief.

Chitra-bhasha—Paintings—or sometimes line drawings.

Cho-pen (Tibetan)—Five-leaved crown used by monks for special services.

Chunam—Lime plaster. Stucco used for sculpture.

Churi—Knife.

Cintamani—Flaming pearl.

Dah-dar (Tibetan)—Divining arrow used in demon worship.

Damaru—Drum.

Danda—Staff.

Devadasi—Temple dancer.

Devalokas—The thirteen heavens of the gods.

Devata—Divinity.

Dharani—A spell or magical prayer in Vajrayana Buddhism.

Dharmachakra—Wheel of life. Wheel of law. Emblem of Buddha's dharma or law.

Dharmakaya—Abstract body of law in Trikaya doctrine.

Dhatu—Relics.

Dhoti—Loincloth worn by Hindus.
Dhvaja—Banner.
Dhyana—Yoga meditation. Descriptive verse for making icons.
Dipalakshmi—Temple lamp in female form.
Dvarpala—Guardian of temple door.
Gada—Mace.
Gahu (Tibetan)—Amulet.
Gaja—Elephant.
Gajasimha—Mythical monster—part lion, part elephant.
Ghanta—Bell.
Ghats—Mountains—or steps on river bank, used for bathing etc.
Gram-devata—Village deity.
Gumpha—Monastery. Cave.
Guru—Teacher.
Hamsa—Goose or swan. Emblem of Brahma. In Buddhism, symbol of the spreading of Buddhist knowledge.
Hara—Necklace or garland.
Hinayana—Small Vehicle. Orthodox sect. Early Buddhism, based on doctrine, rather than Buddha worship.
Isvara—Lord or supreme deity.
Jainism—Religious sect, offshoot of Hinduism, founded by Mahavira in 6th century B.C.—forbids the taking of life.
Jali—Perforated stone screen.
Janabhara—Lemon.
Jata—Hair style—matted.
Jatabanda—Hair style—tying or rolling matted hair, sometimes in a band.
Jataka—Legends of the previous lives of Buddha.
Jata-mukutu—Matted hair, formed in a conical shape.
Kalasa—Water vessel. Rain vase. Container of elixir of life.
Kalpa—Cycle of time.
Kalpalata (Kalpadruma)—Wishing tree.
Kanjur—Soft limestone, used at Taxila (local name).
Karma—Assessment of acts in previous existences, prior to reincarnation.
Karttrka—Chopper.
Karuna—Compassion.
Kaya—Body.
Kesa—Hair—unmatted.
Kesabanda—Hair style.
Khadga—Sword.
Khakkhara—Alarm staff.
Khatvanga—Ritual wand.

Kirtimukh—Lion mask, grotesque.
Kshatriya—Hindu princely or warrior caste.
Kumbha—Vase.
Kundalas—Ear ornaments.
Kusa—Grass for sprinkling nectar.
Laksana—One of 32 marks of the Buddha (anatomical). Symbol or attribute. Detailed formulae of measurement of icons.
Lama—The Superior One. Tibetan monk. Of superior learning. Head of monastery.
Lat—Pillar favoured by Asoka.
Lingam—Phallic symbol of Siva.
Loka—Place or region.
Lota—Water bottle.
Madhayama—The middle proportion of measurement of images.
Mahapurusa—Great person.
Mahayana—The Great Vehicle. Unorthodox sect of Buddhism, later development from the Lesser Vehicle, with emphasis on the worship of Buddhas and Bodhisattvas.
Makara—Mythical fish, similar to crocodile—emblem of water.
Mala—Rosary.
Mandala—Magic circle or diagram. Imagined shape of the cosmos—Buddhist.
Mangala—Jain auspicious symbols.
Mani—Prayers, usually on rolls of paper.
Mani chho khor (Tibetan)—Prayer wheel.
Mantras—Prayer formula. Sacred verse, magic.
Mantrayana—Spell vehicle.
Manusibuddha—Mortal Buddha.
Maya—The ability of gods to assume different forms.
Mayura—Peacock.
Mayurapiccha—Peacock feathers.
Meru—The world mountain of Indian cosmology.
Mithuna—Couple in erotic pose or loving embrace.
Moksha—Transmigration.
Mukatas—Coronets worn by deities.
Mukha—Face.
Mukti—Salvation.
Murti—Epiphany of God—icon—sculpture.
Nadanta—Siva's dance as Nataraja.
Nagara—Capital or city.
Nakula—Mongoose.
Namaskara mudra—Prayer.

Navagraha—The nine planets.
Nayika—Heroine.
Nirmanakaya—The illusion of form of mortal body, assumed by Buddha for the benefit of men (Trikaya doctrine).
Nirvana—Spiritual liberation. Death of the Buddha. Transmigration.
Pada—Foot position. Step.
Padma—Lotus.
Parasu—Axe.
Pasa—Noose.
Patra—Begging bowl.
Phurbu (Tibetan)—Ceremonial triangular dagger, same as dorje.
Pitaka—Container for religious writings.
Pitha—Plinth, base of icon.
Prabha—Halo or arch surrounding figure of deity.
Prana—Breath of life.
Pratibimba—Term used in Indian art, meaning a reconstruction of the hypothetical shape of celestial regions or cosmos in architectural form.
Preta—Demon.
Puja—Worship. Ceremony.
Puranas—Sacred books of Hindu mythology, eighteen in number. In addition there are secondary puranas, which include the Ramayana and the Mahabharata.
Purnaghata—Auspicious symbol. Water vessel.
Pustaka—Book.
Ragmala—String of melodies—Hindu art motif.
Rasa—Idea of beauty—experience communicated by artists. Aesthetic feeling.
Rasleelas—Dances of Krishna with Gopis.
Rath—Temple. Chariot. Term used to describe Pallava shrines.
Ratna—Jewel.
Rishi—Sage. Composer of Vedic hymns. Saint.
Rupakaya—Visible manifestation of a deity or Buddha.
Saddharma Pundarika—Mahayana literature containing the doctrinal essentials of the Great Vehicle. 'The Lotus of Good Law'.
Sadhana—Meditation, used to evoke a deity.
Saktas—A sect which worships only female deities.
Sakti—Active force of a god, expressed as a feminine manifestation. His consort.
Sala (Vatica Robusta)—Indian tree.

Salabhañjika—Hindu art motif: girl touching tree.
Salagrams—Shells associated with Vishnu.
Sama—Position of legs in an icon.
Samadhi—Yoga meditation of deepest form.
Sambhogakaya—Shape in which Buddha reveals himself to Bodhisattvas (Trikaya doctrine).
Samghati—Robes worn by Buddhist monks, and originally by the Buddha.
Samsara—The eternal cycle of life and re-birth.
Sangharma—Buddhist monastery.
Sannyasin—Religious mendicant—Hindu.
Sara—Arrow.
Sastra—Text of rules appertaining to painting, architecture, sculpture or craft. Manuals of law and learning.
Shankha—Conch shell, associated with Vaishnavite deities.
Silpasastra—Text book on sculpture and painting.
Silpin—Mason and sculptor. Craftsman.
Simha—Lion—ornament or motif.
Simhanada—Voice of lion.
Simhasana—Lion throne.
Si-nen (Tibetan)—Metal cymbals used in services.
Siraschakra—Halo behind head of deity.
Sirastraka—Ancient turban.
Skandas—Senses.
Sthanaka-murti—Standing figure.
Stupa—Buddhist relic—shrine or mound.
Sung-ta (Tibetan)—Horoscope.
Sutradhara—Architect.
Svabhava—Self-existent.
Svastika—Swastika.
Svayambhu—Self-creative.
Syana-murti—Reclining figure.
Tandava—Dance of Siva in burning-ghats (cremation ground), symbolic of his power of creation and destruction.
Thang-ka (Thanka) (Tibetan)—Scroll picture. Banner. Sacred picture.
Tantrayana—Buddhist sect, worshippers of female deities.
Tapas—Concentrated energy generated by the gods for creation. In yoga, the practice of exercises aimed at raising humans to the divine or cosmic level.
Tarjani mudra—Manacing.
Thalam—Iconographic length measurement. The palm. Distance from brow to chin.
Tilakam—Mark on forehead.

Trailokya—Three worlds.

Trikaya—In Mahayana Buddhism, the doctrine of the three bodies of Buddha.

Trikona—Triangle.

Trimurti—Three bodies or forms, e.g., Brahma, Vishnu, Siva.

Triratna—Symbol of three jewels—the Buddha, the doctrine and the order.

Trisula—Trident emblem of Siva.

Tshog-shing (Tibetan)—Tanka illustrating assembly of gods of the Tibetan Pantheon.

Upanishads—Ancient religious text.

Urddhvapatta—Buddhist memorial stele.

Urna—Lock of hair or jewel between the eyebrows of Buddha.

Usnisa—Protruberance of the Buddha's head.

Utpala—Blue lotus.

Vahana—Vehicle, mount or accompanying animal of deity. The familiar of the deity.

Vajra—Thunderbolt. The destroying but indestructible emblem of Buddhist and Hindu deities. Diamond.

Vajradhatu Mandala—Magical diagram of the spiritual world (Buddhist).

Vajrasana—The diamond throne of Buddha.

Vajrayana—Buddhist sect. Vehicle of the Thunderbolt. Worshippers and believers in mysticism, etc.

Vanamala—Garland of flowers worn by Vishnu.

Vastusastra—Architectural text book.

Veda—The four religious text books of Brahmanic priestly ritual. The Rig Veda, the most famous of these, was composed in the 1st millennium B.C.

Vedangas—Appendix to the Vedas. Rules of ceremonials, etc.

Vedi—Sacrificial altar.

Vedic—Brahmanic, appertaining to the Vedas.

Vihara—Buddhist monastery.

Vina—Lute.

Visvavajra—Double or crossed thunderbolt.

Vyali—See *Yali*.

Yab-yum (Tibetan)—Father-Mother.

Yajna—Sacrificial fire. Sacrifice.

Yajnapavita—Sacred thread worn by Brahmins.

Yalis—Fantastic monsters—lions with elephants' trunks.

Yantras—Mystic amuletic diagrams.

Yoga—System of meditation and self-control for spiritual realisation. Communication with universal spirit.

Yogapatta—The band used for supporting the knees in the

yogasana.

Yogi—One who practises yoga.

Yupa—Sacrificial post.

BIBLIOGRAPHY

Archer, W. G.	Bazaar Paintings of Calcutta. (Her Majesty's Stationery Office and Victoria and Albert Museum, London, 1953)
Archer, W. G.	Kalighat Drawings. (Marg Publications, Bombay, 1962)
Archer, W. G.	Indian Painting in the Punjab Hills. (London, 1952)
Archer, W. G.	Kangra Painting. (London, 1952)
Archer, W. G.	Garhwal Painting. (London, 1954)
Archer, W. G.	Indian Painting. (Oxford U. Press, 1957).
Archer, W. G.	Central Indian Painting. (London, 1958)
Archer, W. G.	Paintings of the Sikhs. (London, 1966)
Archer, Mildred and Archer, W. G.	Indian Painting for the British, 1770–1880. (Oxford, 1955)
Archer, W. G.	Indian Miniatures. (New York Graphic Society)
Barrett, D.	Sculptures from Amaravati. (In the British Museum)
Basham, A. L.	The Wonder That Was India. (Grove, 1959)
Coomaraswamy, A. K.	Rajput Painting. (Oxford, 1916)
Frederic, Louis	Indian Temples and Sculpture. (Thames & Hudson, 1959)
Goetz, H.	India—Five Thousand Years of Indian Art. (Baden-Baden, 1959)
Gordon, Antoinette K.	The Iconography of Tibetan Lamaism. (Paragon, 1967)
Gray, B. and Barrett, D.	Painting of India. (Skira)

Randhawa, M. S.   Kangra Valley Painting.
                      (New Delhi, 1954)
Randhawa, M. S.   Basohli Painting.
                      (Verry, 1959)
Randhawa, M. S.   Kangra Paintings of the Bhagavata
                      Purana.
                      (New Delhi, 1960)
Randhawa, M. S.   Kangra Paintings on Love.
                      (New Delhi, 1962)
Randhawa, M. S.   Kangra Paintings of the Gita
                      Govinda.
                      (New Delhi, 1963)
Randhawa, M. S.   Kangra Paintings of the Bihari
                      Sat Sai.
                      (Verry, 1966)
Rawson, P.   Indian Painting.
                      (London, Paris and New York, 1961)
Rawson, P.   Indian Sculpture.
                      (Dutton Vista, 1966)
Rowland, B.   The Art and Architecture of India.
                      (Penguin, 1953)
Saraswati, S. K.   A Survey of Indian Sculpture.
                      (Mukhopadhyay, 1957)
Saraswati, S. K.   Early Sculpture of Bengal.
                      (Sambodhi Publications,
                        2nd Edition, 1962)
Singh, Madanjeet   Indian Miniatures.
  (Photographs)   (New York Graphic Society)
Smith, Vincent   Fine Art in India and Ceylon.
                      (Bombay)
Thapar, D. R.   Icons in Bronze.
                      (Bombay, 1961)
Waddell, L. A.   The Buddhism of Tibet—
                      or Lamaism.
                      (Cambridge, 1967)
Wheeler, M.   The Indus Civilisation.
                      (Cambridge University, 1953,
                        3rd Edition, 1968)
Zimmer, Heinrich   The Art of Indian Asia.
                      (Princeton U. Press, 1960)
                      Designs in the Traditional Arts of
                      Bengal.
                      (Director of Industries, Government
                      of West Bengal)

Chart of symbols used on images

1 Arrow	— *Sara*	7 Bowl	— *Patra*		
2 Axe	— *Parasu*	8 Chisel	— *Tanka*		
3 Banner	— *Dhvaja*	9 Chopper	— *Karttrka*		
4 Bell	— *Ghanta*	10 Conch	— *Sankha*		
5 Book	— *Pustaka*	11 Dagger	— *Phurbu*		
6 Bow	— *Capa*	12 Drum	— *Damaru*		
13 Feathers	— *Mayurapiccha*	19 Goad (elephant)	— *Ankusa*		
14 Flame	— *Agni*	20 Horse	— *Lung-ta*		
15 Flower	— *Asoka*	21 Jewel	— *Ratna*		
16 Flower	— *Campa*	22 Jewels (three)	— *Triratna*		
17 Flywhisk	— *Camara*	23 Knife	— *Churi*		
18 Fruit	— *Myrobalan*	24 Lemon	— *Jambhara*		
25 Lotus	— *Utpala*	31 Noose	— *Pasa*		
26 Lotus	— *Padma*	32 Ornaments (apron)	— *Sanmudras*		
27 Lute	— *Vina*	33 Parasol	— *Atapatra*		
28 Mace	— *Gada*	34 Pearl	— *Cintamani*		
29 Mongoose	— *Nakula*	35 Plough	— *Hala*		
30 Moon	— *Candra*	36 Reliquary	— *Caitya*		
37 Rosary	— *Mala*	43 Sun	— *Surya*		
38 Serpent	— *Naga*	44 Swastika	— *Swastika*		
39 Skull cup	— *Kapala*	45 **Sword**	— *Khadga*		
40 Spear	— *Sakti*	46 Thunderbolt	— *Vajra*		
41 Staff	— *Khakkhara*	47 Thunderbolt	— *Visvajra*		
42 Staff	— *Danda*	48 Triangle	— *Trikona*		

49 Trident	— *Trisula*
50 Vase	— *Kalasa*
51 Wheel	— *Cakra*

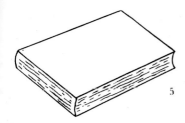

5

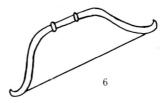

6

7

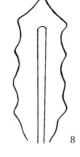

8

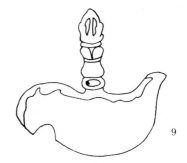

9

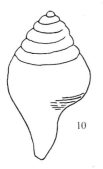

10

11

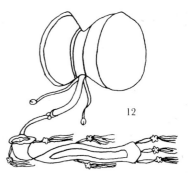

12

13

14

15

16

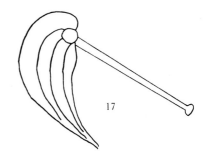

17

18

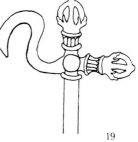

19

20

21

22

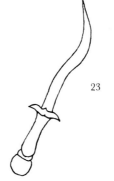

23

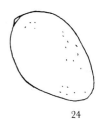

24

25

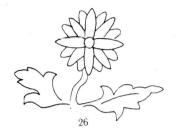

26

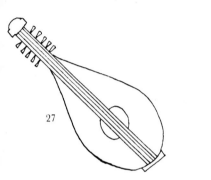

27

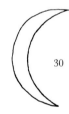

28

30

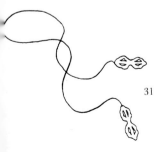

29

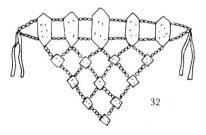

31

32

33

34

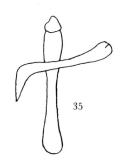

35

36

37

38

39

40

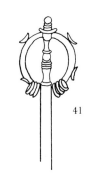

41

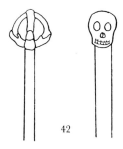

42

172

43

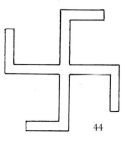

44

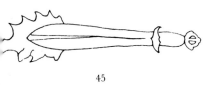

45

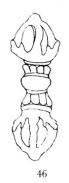

46

47

48

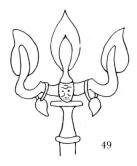

49

50

51

173

Examples of Hair Styles
and Headdresses

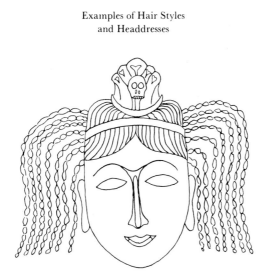

Jata Bandha

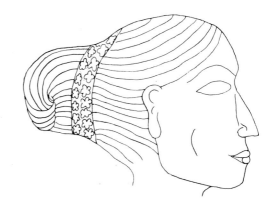

Kesa Bandha

Jata Bandha

Kirita-Mukuta

Karanda-Mukuta

175

Jata-Mukuta

Eight glorious emblems shown in two styles

1 Conch
2 White parasol
3 Standard
4 Two fishes

5 Lotus
6 Vase
7 Endless knot
8 Wheel

1

2

3

4

177

5

6

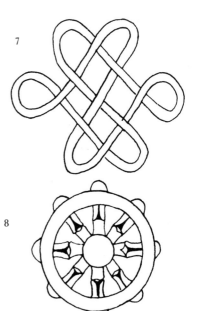

7

8

1 a–d	Indo-Persian Style; *c.* 1503–5.
2	Mughal-Akbar Period; *c.* 1600.
3	Mughul—Shah Jehan Period; *c.* 1630.
4	Deccan; mid-17th century.
5	C. India, Malwa; mid-16th century.
6a & 6b	Rajasthan Mewar; *c.* 1605.
7	Rajasthan—Bundi; *c.* 1680.
8	Rajasthan—Bundi; *c.* 1780.
9	Provincial Mughal (Oudh); mid-18th century.
10	Provincial Mughal—Murshidabad; mid-18th century.
11	Rajasthan—Jaisalmer; early 18th century.
12	Rajasthan—Bikaner; *c.* 1800.
13	Rajasthan—Jodhpur; mid-18th century.
14	Rajasthan—Kishangarh; *c.* 1770.
16	Rajasthan—Jaipur; *c.* 1780.
15	Punjab Hills—Basohli; *c.* 1680.
17	Punjab Hills—Basohli; *c.* 1720.
18a & 18b	Punjab Hills—Basohli; *c.* 1730.
19	Pubjab Hills—Nurpur; *c.* 1710.
20	Punjab Hills—Kulu; *c.* 1700.
21	Punjab Hills—Jammu; *c.* 1760.
22	Punjab Hills—Jammu; *c.* 1770.
23	Punjab Hills—Guler; 1765.
24	Punjab Hills—Guler; 1800.
25	Punjab Hills—Kangra; 1790.
26	Punjab Hills—Kangra; 1790.
27	Punjab Hills—Garhwal; 1785.

1a

1b

1c

1d

2

3

4

5

6a

6b

7

8

9

10

11

12

13

14

15

16

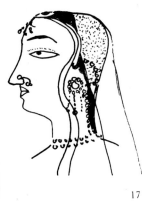

17

18a

18b

183

19   20   21a

21b   22   23

26

24   25   27

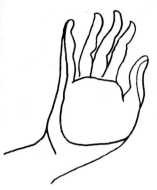
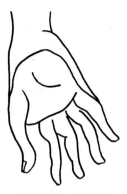

ABHAYA   VARADA or VARA   BHUMISPARSA

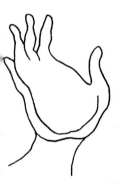

ANJALI

NAMASKARA

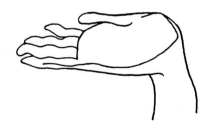

BHUTADAMARA   BUDDHASRAMANA

185

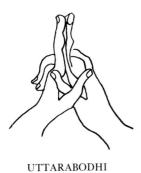

UTTARABODHI

DHYANA or SAMADHI

KARANA

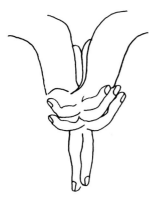

KSEPANA

VAJRAHUMKARA

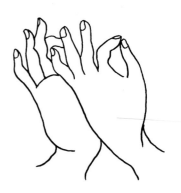

TRIPATAKA

ARDHA-CHANDRA

DHARMACAKRA

186

VISMAYA

TARJANI

TARPANA

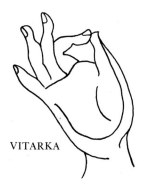

VITARKA

187

INDEX

192